The Efficacy of Financial Structures for Islamic Ta
Proceedings of the 7th AMI Contemporary Fiqhī I

Proceedings of the AMI Contemporary Fiqhī Issues Workshop

VOLUME 1

The Efficacy of Financial Structures for Islamic Taxes and Dues

Proceedings of the 7th AMI Contemporary Fiqhī Issues Workshop
4–5th July, 2019

Edited by

Wahid M. Amin

AMI PRESS

THE EFFICACY OF FINANCIAL STRUCTURES FOR ISLAMIC TAXES AND DUES
PROCEEDINGS OF THE 7th AMI CONTEMPORARY FIQHĪ ISSUES WORKSHOP, 4–5th JULY 2019

ISBN 978-1-8380320-0-5

Printed in the United Kingdom

CONTENTS

List of Contributors vii

Introduction: The Efficacy of Financial Structures for Islamic Taxes and Dues 1

Wahid M. Amin

A Functional Interpretation of *Zakāt* and the Inclusion of Contemporary Taxation as Its Legitimate Form 8

Arif Abdul Hussain

Prophetic Initiatives to Institutionalise Money Matters: An Historical Overview through al-Kittānī's *al-Tarātīb al-idāriyya* 33

Ahmed Saad al-Azhari al-Hasani

Religious Tax as a Source of Income for Religious Study: A New Approach towards the Problem and Its Solution 49

Ali Fanaei

Reviving *Ta'līf*: Strategic Charity to Counter the Rise of the Far Right 63

Jaffer Ladak

List of Contributors

Wahid M. Amin

received his DPhil in Islamic Philosphy from the University of Oxford in 2017 and is currently a lecturer at the Al-Mahdi Institute. He has published on a variety of subjects in the history of post-Avicennan philosophy. Since 2018 he has also served as the Head of Publishing at AMI Press, and is currently working on a major collobarative project on the *Collected Writings of al-ʿAllāma al-Ḥillī*, a multi-volume series of English translations and studies of key works by the medieval Imāmī scholar al-Ḥasan ibn Yūsuf ibn Mutahhar al-Ḥillī (d. 726/1325). The series is being published by AMI Press over the course of the next five years.

Arif Abdul Hussain

is the director and founder of the Al-Mahdi Institute, where he lectures in *uṣūl al-fiqh* and philosophy. He has been at the forefront of developing and delivering advanced Islamic studies in the UK and has been lecturing on Islam for over twenty years, having in the process attained an international reputation as one of the most critical thinkers in the contemporary Muslim world. He is also the author of the *Islam and God-centricity* series, a collection of works exploring the author's own existential philosophy and its application across a wide variety of theological and legal issues in Islam.

Ahmed Saad al-Azhari al-Hasani

is a graduate of Al-Azhar University and the founder and director of the Ihsan Institute in the UK. Having trained under such esteemed scholars as the Grand Mufti of Egypt Shaykh Ali Gomaa, Shaykh Habib Abu Bakr al-Mashhur and Shaykh Habib Umar bin Hafiz, he was appointed the Imam of North London Central Mosque in 2007, the same mosque that had previously gained notoriety because of the extremist preacher Abu Hamza al-Misri. He is the author of numerous publications, including *Contemplating the Quran: A Thematic Thirty Part Commentary on the Noble Quran* which was published in 2017.

Ali Fanaei

received his PhD in Philosophy from the University of Sheffield after having completed 17 years of seminary studies at the Hawza Ilmiyya of Qom where he attended advanced sessions taught by leading experts such as Ayatollah Mohaghegh Damad, Ayatollah Tabrizi, Ayatollah Ha'iri, Ayatollah Wahid Khorasani, Ayatollah Montazeri, and Ayatollah Ahmad Mianeji. Alongside his teaching activities at the Al-Mahdi Institute and Mofid University of Qom, he is the author of numerous publications in English and Farsi. Dr. Fanaei is currently regarded as one of the leading figures of the *rowshan fikrī* ('enlightenment thinkers') school and has made several appearances on broadcast media in Iran.

Jaffer Ladak

is the Resident Alim of Hujjat Stanmore, London. He has spoken at numerous locations around the world and is a committed social activist who has appeared on numerous TV and social media outlets. He is currently a student at the Al-Mahdi Institute having previously trained at the Islamic seminaries of Ayatollah al-Qazwini and Ayatollah Sayyid Taqi al-Modarresi in Karbala, Iraq.

WAHID M. AMIN

Introduction: The Efficacy of Financial Structures for Islamic Taxes and Dues

In 2013 the Al-Mahdi Institute (AMI) held its first Contemporary Fiqhī Issues Workshop exploring the jurisprudence of fasting and has since continued each year to organise what has now become an annual workshop recognised by Islamic law specialists throughout the world. The aim of these workshops is to provide a platform for scholarly exchange in the widest possible sense of the term, bringing together under one roof scholars from both traditional seminary and other academic and professional backgrounds to discuss and debate topics within Islamic law. As such, the AMI Contemporary Fiqhī Issues Workshop provides a forum unlike any other in the academic world. And although at times the epistemic assumptions may vary considerably among participants, it is these very differences that make for enriching discussion and debate. Such trend-setting initiatives encapsulate the ethos of the Al-Mahdi Institute since it was founded in 1993 to make the study of Islam a non-territorial space of scholarship that engages experts no matter what their background, recognising that the study of Islam has no one set methodology or privileged community of scholars. Over the years, the Institute has held workshops covering a broad range of topics including family law, human rights, the status of non-Muslims, violence in Sharia, and the history and future of Shīʿī *ijtihād*, with participants from many of these gatherings going on to publish their research in books and journals with an international readership.

As guest editor of this volume it gives me immense pleasure to not only introduce the exciting papers that fill its pages, but also to write the introduction of the first officially published proceedings volume of the AMI Contemporary Fiqhī Issues Workshop. The papers gathered in this volume represent the contributions of some of the participants of the 7th Contemporary Fiqhī Issues Workshop that was held at the Al-Mahdi Institute on 4–5th July 2019. The theme of the workshop focussed on the efficacy of financial structures for Islamic taxes and dues and aimed to provide participants the opportunity to critically evaluate the financial mechanisms and wealth management strategies within Islamic law. For over a millennium, Islamic law has institutionalised money (and other economic assets) to implement its vision of a just society. Be it religious taxation in the form of *zakāt*, charitable donations in the form of *ṣadaqa* or religious endowments (*awqāf*), the dowry that is paid by a man to his would-be wife in a marriage contract, or the different categories of financial compensation within Islamic criminal and tort law, the Sharia utilises money and wealth for a diverse range of functions and objectives. Some of these assume a functioning political framework involving government officials and an Islamic judiciary system, while others seem to be effective only in the pre-modern contexts in which they were conceived and implemented. In the contemporary age, Muslims live under different models of government that range from Islamic governments such as the Islamic Republic of Iran to secular states such as the United Kingdom, each with their own financial structures. In the West, Muslims are already subjected to a variety of state taxes, many of which are used for the same welfare objectives as traditional Islamic taxes, which raises interesting questions about the need and efficacy of further Islamic taxation in addition to these other forms of tax already paid by Muslim citizens of the secular state. The papers in this volume therefore engage the topic of religious taxation in Islam from a wide range of philosophical, sociological, ethical, historical, and cultural perspectives, each offering unique insights and perspectives on the possibility of financial structures within Islamic law developing and evolving with the times and in accordance with different models of government.

The papers that are presented here focus on the laws of religious taxation – i.e. *zakāt* and *khums* – from different ends and perspectives of the jurisprudential discussion surrounding them. The possibility that *zakāt* may be levied on categories beyond those that are traditionally recognised as being subject to the law of *zakāt* is considered by Arif Abdul Hussain in his paper entitled 'A Functional Interpretation of *Zakāt* and the Inclusion of Contemporary Taxation as Its legitimate Form'. Traditional Islamic jurisprudence (*fiqh*) does not consider an individual's salaried income to be a *zakāt*-able entity. A brief glance at the kinds of entities most *fuqahā'* consider to be subject to religious taxation in fact reveals that what is primarily taxable in this regard is not the salaried income a person earns through labour, but rather the material possessions they own over the course of a financial year, the majority of which are ostensibly linked to farming and agricultural economies. *Zakāt* is thus levied form of taxation on material commodities (*amwāl*) such as grazing livestock, gold and silver, and different types of grain such as wheat and barley. Apart from these there is no religious taxation in the form of *zakāt*, which raises the question of whether or not *zakāt* as a fiscal policy is an outmoded form of religious taxation in the modern world. Whereas in the Prophetic era the burden of religious taxation would have fallen on the shoulders of a mainly agrarian populace, the same tax traditionally-conceived it seems appears only fully applicable to a small segment of the UK population today in an economy which, since the nineteenth-century, has rapidly moved toward industrialisation away from agriculture-based economies. One can see this in the very fact that organisations that collect *zakāt* taxes from Muslims in the UK, for example, do so on the monetary value of gold and silver, the other categories being more or less redundant. Arif Abdul Hussain's contribution therefore challenges two crucial aspects of the traditional law of *zakāt* by arguing that not only should the taxes a person pays on their income (e.g. in the UK) be considered legitimate instances of religious taxation, but also – and perhaps even more controversially – that these may be legitimately handed over to a 'secular' state without undermining their 'religious' status even if the recipients of these taxes are non-Muslims. To justify such a radically ground-shifting perspective, the author urges us to reconceptualise the notion of *zakāt* in accordance with a functionalist paradigm in which the emphasis lies not so much on the *form* of *zakāt* but its essence, that is to say, the outcomes and purposes for which *zakāt* is striving. This is further elaborated on the basis of the author's 'existentialist philosophy' whereby religious norms are measured against the overarching purpose and philosophy of a human being's existence, which is to maximise growth both at the individual and collective level. The legal norms of Islam are thus regarded to be productive to the extent that they are facilitative causes for the growth of the human individual and their society; it is this that defines their 'Islamic' character or essence and not the historical formulation of the laws themselves. Hence, given that the legal definition of *ṣalāt* would have necessarily had to change when the *qibla* of the Muslims changed from Jerusalem to Mecca in the Prophetic era, this does not imply that the essence of *ṣalāt* would have also had to change. While the form of a legal norm is susceptible to change over time in differing contexts, the essence of what the norm strives after is eternal and changeless. It is on this meta-legal understanding of the nature of legal norms that Abdul Hussain argues that the form of *zakāt* can also change under different circumstances all the while preserving the essence of the law of *zakāt*, which is to distribute wealth in a just manner to facilitate the moral, spiritual and intellectual growth of the members of society whatever their religious beliefs so long as they are not hostile to Muslims or the religion of Islam.

Ahmed Saad al-Azhari al-Hasani's contribution 'Prophetic Initiatives to Institutionalise Money Matters: An Historical Overview through Al-Kittānī's *al-Tarātīb al-idāriyya*' examines the historical origins of pre-Islamic notions of charity and the guidelines found within the Prophet Muḥammad's own processes for administering *zakāt*, tax, land revenue and charity collection by offering a close reading of Sayyid ʿAbd al-Ḥayy ibn ʿAbd al-Kabīr al-Kittānī's (d. 1962) work, *al-Tarātīb al-idāriyya*. This detailed work provides both a clear historical understanding of the Prophet's role as the head of state as well as the administrative framework he introduced for the collection and distribution of different forms of state revenue, from which al-Hasani argues there are instructional guidelines and strategies for the effective management of collected taxes for modern-day Muslim states. The author begins by first introducing the philanthropic nature of the pre-Islamic Arabs, and in doing so highlights the importance of charitable acts for social distinction and reputation among individuals and tribal classes. With the establishment of Medina as the first Islamic city-state, however, the act of giving charity had to be reformulated by means of a shift in cultural practices, so that in order to sustain the growth of the community an individual's act of charity was now facilitated by means of a centralised authority in the form of a mandatory levied tax. As such, the law of *zakāt* became a fully-fledged state-administered tax which built on the social norms and customs of pre-Islamic Arabian society, and with it came the introduction of entirely new systems for fiscal management that were unprecedented in traditional Arabian culture. Al-Hasani's chapter outlines in detail the variety of roles and positions that were created through Prophetic initiatives to manage public money; initiatives that were designed to administer public funds in the most efficacious and transparent way. Al-Hasani identifies three major areas in which such initiatives were undertaken: (1) resources, (2) funds and (3) spending. Initiatives linked to resources were primarily designed for the purpose of calculating the amount of religious taxation from assets such as crops and grazing animals, and in the process required specialisation in three subsidiary functions, namely, estimation, documentation, and role-creation. Once funds were collected, this in turn led to other Prophetic initiatives to preserve and supervise fiscal management, before finally being spent in financially prudent and responsible ways. The state functionaries and official posts that were therefore introduced through Prophetic initiatives were all designed to ensure minimal wastage in the system, full accountability and documentation at every stage, and proper administration of public funds so that the most deserving members of society could receive state support. As al-Hasani remarks, such 'Prophetic initiatives to institutionalise public money in his city-state of Medina were creative and unprecedented'.

Although Islam encourages charity and religious taxation through financial structures such as *ṣadaqa* and *zakāt*, the management and distribution of funds gathered by charitable organisations and/or central authorities (where applicable) is not an uncomplicated affair. Furthermore, Shīʿī *fiqh* imposes a specific kind of religious tax known as *khums*, the one-fifth tax, which in the modern context is almost exclusively restricted to an individual's profits from earnings barring any sudden discoveries of treasure troves or precious minerals obtained from underwater diving (in which case one would also have to pay *khums* on these too). Unlike *zakāt*, the *khums* levy can only be distributed to *sayyid*s who are poor, or who are orphans, or who have become stranded on a journey; or to a division of *khums* known as the *sahm al-imām*, the portion reserved for the Twelfth Imam which, in the present circumstances of the Imam's occultation, must either be given to a qualified *mujtahid* or to those whom he (invariably male) has authorised. In fact, many jurists even specify that the *mujtahid* in question be the most learned *marjaʿ* of the age, which restricts the number of people who are responsible for such vast sums of money to a relatively small handful of individuals. It is impossible to estimate how much money is accumulated through *khums* each year given the lack of transparency and public accounting.

One of the ways in which this money is spent is for the religious education and training of scholars enrolled at the Shīʿī seminaries of Iran and Iraq. Aside from the questions this raises concerning the use of funds when religion and state politics overlap, a specific problem arises with respect to the individuals themselves who are conducting supposedly 'independent' research but whose source of income relies on payments from the state (or *marjaʿ*) that have been derived from religious taxation. The question of whether or not this leads to a conflict of interest is raised and discussed in Ali Fanaei's paper as part of a wider conversation with two previous scholars' views on the subject: Ayatollah Morteza Motahhari and Abdulkarim Soroush. Fanaei begins by summarising each of these authors' opinions, noting how that even though both considered there to be a problem in the way money was managed for religious education, they nonetheless disagreed on the diagnosis of where the problem lay exactly and what its solution(s) ought to be. Indeed, although Motahhari acknowledged the possibility of a conflict of interest, he did not believe the problem to be an insurmountable one; whereas in the case of Soroush, the problem is fundamentally irreconcilable. However, according to Soroush, the conflict is a much more deeply rooted one than Motahhari had conceived, and has less to do with whether or not a scholar's research depends on money that is derived from religious taxation, but instead on the very fact that the 'clergy' rely on religion as their source of income. Soroush therefore argues for a distinction between the clergy (i.e. individuals who rely on religion for their income), on the one hand, and religious scholars who investigate religion without depending on it for their income. In other words, a religious scholar (as opposed to the clergyman) is someone who has an independent source of income which, according to Soroush, guarantees that his research on religion and his source of income do not get intermingled in a conflict of interest. For Soroush, the problem therefore lies in the intermingling of religion as an object of study and investigation and religion as a source of income, and the remedy to this problem ought to lie unsurprisingly in a complete and total separation between them. Fanaei rejects Soroush's solution to the problem and rejects both his and Motahhari's identification of where the problem lies exactly in the first instance. As Fanaei shows, the conflict of interest is a moral problem with epistemic consequences in religious and non-religious scholarship, and hence is not specifically a problem confined to religious studies only. A scientist whose source of income relies on science is not necessarily conflicted. The solution that Fanaei offers is more holistic than either of the solutions provided by Motahhari and Soroush given the multifaceted nature of the problem, and includes taking steps at the economic, social and political levels to ensure that misconduct is eliminated wherever possible.

In the final contribution of this volume, Jaffer Ladak makes a strong argument in favour of spending *zakāt* funds as a means of resisting the rise of far-right movements in the UK which have a detrimental impact on Muslims living in this country and on the image of Islam more generally. The potential scope for doing this already exists, suggests Ladak, within the *fiqh* of *zakāt* itself, especially in the notion that *zakāt* may be legitimately distributed in order to persuade 'those whose hearts are inclined' (*al-mu'allafa qulūbuhum*). Traditionally, this was understood to mean that the wealth that was generated through *zakāt* could be distributed (1) to help those of weak *īmān* from leaving the faith of Islam altogether or (2) to win the allegiance and military services of disbelievers who could be employed to fight against the combatant enemies of the Muslim community. *Ta'līf* was thus a fiscal mechanism of ensuring the survival of the Islamic faith, especially in the Prophetic period when the religion of Islam was still at its early developmental stages and as such exposed to threats from both within and without the Muslim community. Nowadays, although Islam is a global religion and as such does not face any imminent threat of extinction, it is this very success of Islam and its 'intrusion' onto the global scene which agitates Islamophobes everywhere. As shown by Ladak, the statistics measuring the rise of far-right movements in the UK and Islamophobic hate speech and violence make for shocking reading. As a way of counteracting these tendencies, Ladak proposes the use of the notion of *ta'līf* as a form of 'strategic spending' so that a positive public image of Muslims and the Islamic religion is created, whereby Muslim charities and taxes are used to feed poor white working-class children in UK town and cities. It is often areas like these where poverty among the young white working-class population provides a strong breeding ground for far-right propaganda and recruitment. By targeting these demographic areas strategically and implementing policies that help the local white population appreciate the contribution of their fellow Muslim citizens, there lies the possibility that many misconceptions and deliberate misrepresentations of Islam and Muslims could be debunked and dispelled within the very communities where such negative discourses are prevalent.

As demonstrated by the papers collected in this volume, research on the efficacy of financial structures for Islamic taxes and dues raises important questions about the theory and practice of money-matters in Islam. From the very philosophical foundations of *zakāt* that define its nature and purpose to the practical ways in which these funds are administered and distributed, the papers in this proceeding's volume each show how vibrant and multifaceted the discussion on religious taxation and dues can be within Muslim jurisprudential discourse. Furthermore, as the authors of these timely papers demonstrate, the debates and discussions on religious taxation are no longer just confined to the narrow context of Muslim society and politics only, but in the modern period naturally involve the consideration of secular authorities and their financial structures – and in some instances their direct involvement also – to inform Muslim jurisprudential discourse on money-matters within Sharia.

As a final word, I would like to thank all those who through their hard work and dedication have made this and each of the previous years' Fiqhī Workshops possible: the organisers and administrators, security and facilities staff, caterers, panel organisers and chairs, IT staff, student volunteers and, of course, all of the speakers and delegates who participated in the workshops. The Institute is blessed to have a team of committed staff, many of whom work tirelessly behind the scenes to ensure the smooth running of the Institute and its activities such as events like the Fiqhī Workshop. It is to them – Rukhsana Bhanji, Ali Redha Khaki, Hashim Bata, Mahdiya Abdul Hussain and Muhammed Reza Tajri (who, by the way, has convened the Fiqhī Workshop in exemplary fashion over the last few years) – that I give the final mention. Thank you for all of your hard work.

ARIF ABDUL HUSSAIN

A Functional Interpretation of *Zakāt* and the Inclusion of Contemporary Taxation as Its Legitimate Form

This paper seeks to ascertain whether it is justifiable to equate the various types of state taxes in the modern era with legitimate instances of *zakāt*. This is because, by and large, they serve the same societal function as *zakāt*, which is to alleviate poverty and cater for societal needs. If this is justifiable, then the Qur'anic obligation of *zakāt* – which is incumbent upon all Muslims – will have been discharged for Muslim taxpayers. To answer this question, an analysis of the notion of *zakāt* in the Qur'an, supplemented by the *ḥadīth* literature, has been conducted to extrapolate its function, or essence, as per the 'existential framework'.[1] Since the occurrence of the word *zakāt* in the Qur'anic verses is predominantly accompanied by the word *ṣalāt* (ritual prayer), this paper also includes analysis of the latter term. Accordingly, an in-depth analysis of the evolution of the forms of both *ṣalāt* and *zakāt* are presented, demonstrating that their respective evolutions were contingent upon maximising the growth of the individual and community in differing societal contexts.[2] The analysis of the former will present its forms as it gradually evolved into the five daily prayers.[3] The analysis of the latter will include the other extensions of taxation that are contingent upon societal need; that is, *khums* and *fay'*. The fact that *ṣalāt* underwent several modifications is important for it will be argued that if the sacrosanct and spiritual obligation of *ṣalāt* needed to be modified, then a

1 The 'existential framework' is a legal methodology developed by the author. For more information, see the 'Academic Articles' section on the author's personal website: https://shaykharif.com/works.

2 The 'form' of an action refers to its practice by the individuals and community. The phrase 'form of *ṣalāt*' refers to the five daily prayers, and it includes their obligatoriness, timings of performance, numbers of units, constituent actions, content to be recited, prerequisites and rules. The phrase 'form of *zakāt*' includes its obligatoriness, subjects, recipients and percentage.

3 This is because, in the Qur'an, whenever the word *ṣalāt* accompanies the word *zakāt*, the former signifies 'daily *ṣalāt*' in the Meccan verses and 'five daily prayers' in the Medinan verses.

fortiori the social obligation of *zakāt* must be subject to ongoing and periodic modification, since it was instituted solely to address societal needs.

Ṣalāt and *zakāt* are spiritual requirements that frequently appear together throughout many verses of the Qur'an, especially within the Medinan chapters. In eight of these verses, the command *aqīmū* (establish) accompanies the word *ṣalāt*, and the command *ātū* (give) precedes the word *zakāt*. Both convey the meaning of obligation: the former, of establishing a prescribed form of prayer; and the latter, of giving wealth to the needy. The words *ṣalāt* and *zakāt* are also used in the Qur'an to refer to practices enjoined upon the prophets preceding the Prophet Muḥammad and the Jews of Medina.[4] Furthermore, the Qur'an emphasises the fact that Ismāʿīl, who was considered by the Arabs as their ancestral prophet, also exhorted certain forms of *ṣalāt* and *zakāt* to his people.[5] This is indicative of the following: firstly, that such practices of bygone peoples also count as extensions of the words *ṣalāt* and *zakāt*; secondly, that such practices have been enjoined upon communities since that time; and thirdly, that enjoining people to *ṣalāt* and *zakāt* was one of the functions of prophethood. One may conclude, therefore, that *ṣalāt* and *zakāt* are salient features of the *dīn* (way or religion) of God that has been revealed to successive prophets, and that their extensions have been practised by the other Abrahamic faiths.[6]

As an intrinsic part of this one dīn of God, *zakāt* is, therefore, presumed to be a special form of levy that cannot be negated under any circumstances. In addition, since the religious obligation of *zakāt* predominantly occurs alongside *ṣalāt* in the Qur'an, it is often understood that both hold equal status as religious obligations; thus, since the latter is immutable, so must the former be as well.[7] However, since it is assumed, and all Muslims will acknowledge, that their

---

4 'And We made them leaders who guided by Our command, and We revealed to them the doing of good and the establishment of prayer and the giving of *zakāt*; and they were worshipful towards Us' (21:73). 'And establish [O children of Isrā'īl] the *ṣalāt* and give the *zakāt*, and bow with those who bow' (2:43). Please note that all Qur'anic translations are the author's own.

5 'And recall in the scripture of Ismā'īl; he was truthful in his promise, and was a messenger, a prophet. He used to call his people to *ṣalāt* and *zakāt*, and he was with his Lord who was pleased with him' (19:54–55).

6 Of course, the Qur'an is clear on this (see, for example, the verses in notes 4 and 5 above); moreover, this has also been suggested by some exegetes of the Qur'an. See, for example, A. B. ʿArabī, *Aḥkām al-Qur'ān* (Beirut: Dār al-Fikr, 2005), 1:34.

7 N. Calder, '*Zakāt* in Imāmī Shīʿī Jurisprudence, from the Tenth to the Sixteenth Century A.D.', *Bulletin of the School of Oriental and African Studies* 44, no. 3 (1981): 468.

different forms were revealed to prophets of every community, the question 'what is immutable in the "Muslim" *ṣalāt* and *zakāt*?' is a significant one. Are the functions of *ṣalāt* and *zakāt* immutable, or their forms? In other words, are the essences of *ṣalāt* and *zakāt* eternal, acontextual, ahistorical and universal, or their forms? For each of these obligations – and indeed every obligatory act – consists of two interdependent but distinct components: function (or essence) and form.[8]

Therefore, the Qur'an presents *ṣalāt* and *zakāt* as having always been spiritual obligations within differing contexts. From this, it can be extrapolated that each must have a spiritual facet that is universal[9] and a societal facet that is contextual[10]; the former constitutes the essence and the latter the form. The existential framework deems this to be the case for every legal regulation (*ḥukm sharʿī*); that is, they all consist of these two elements. The forms of regulations are contingent upon, and bound to, their respective contexts; accordingly, they change and fluctuate in accordance with differing contexts to ensure that the essences of those regulations – which are eternal, acontextual, ahistorical and universal – are secured. This, in turn, warrants that regulations are congruent with the existential state of individuals and communities in order to facilitate their intellectual, moral and spiritual growth. Thus, growth of the individual and community is the foundation and impetus of every regulation; that is, God stipulates regulations that are beneficial or harmful on the basis of growth.[11]

The subsequent sections demonstrate that the essence of *ṣalāt* is to provide individuals with a specified period of intense God-centric orientation so that a God-centric community ensues; and the essence of *zakāt* is to purify the individual from vices and moral inadequacies, to alleviate poverty from society and to accommodate societal needs. The formal aspects of both are formulated on the basis of securing these spiritual–societal essences. It follows, therefore, that the traditional form of *zakāt* will only be valid to the extent that it serves its purpose and accommodates its essence; otherwise, it must be modified so that its purpose, or essence, is secured. This is because the essence of a regulation is universal and immutable, which in the case of *zakāt*, as a levy, is the removal of

8 The philosophical distinctions of form and essence finds precedent in the Qur'anic notions of outer (*ẓāhir*) and inner (*bāṭin*). See S. H. Nasr, ed., *The Study Quran: A New Translation and Commentary* (New York: HarperOne, 2015), 26, 30.

9 That is, it transcends the particularity of time and space.

10 That is, it is bound to a particular time and place.

11 A. Abdul Hussain, *Islam and God-centricity: A Theological Basis for Human Liberation* (Birmingham: Sajjadiyya Press, 2017), 11–15.

poverty and the fulfilment of societal needs. Although there is parity between *ṣalāt* and *zakāt* in terms of spiritual significance and importance in the Qur'an, this does not necessitate parity in the degree of 'formal' modification; one may be subject to greater modification than the other in practice, depending on the demands of the existential context.

1. The Evolution of the Forms of *Ṣalāt* and *Zakāt* in the Qur'an and *Ḥadīth* Literature

The question of whether it is legitimate to consider certain types of state taxes in the modern era as extensions of *zakāt* will be answered by demonstrating that the forms of both *ṣalāt* and *zakāt* underwent several changes in accordance with the fluctuating context of the Prophet Muḥammad. Therefore, this section presents chronologically the introduction of the notions of *ṣalāt* and *zakāt*, and their respective verbal and nominal derivatives, to the nascent audience of the Qur'an; the progressive development of each of their forms, and changes in the utility of their respective verbal and nominal derivatives, as the audience evolved and their context gradually changed; and the culmination of their final forms. It should be noted that the final form of *ṣalāt* is its perfect and complete form (or its universal form) because it caters for the spiritual needs of all individuals of society irrespective of spiritual calibre – that is, it was formulated in light of the lowest common denominator in society. As for *zakāt*, its final form represents the institutionalised levy that was appropriate for the needs of the Medinan society of the Prophet.

The order of revelation delineated here is the traditional chronology accepted by the majority of Muslim scholars.[12]

12 See A. Jaffer and M. Jaffer, *An Introduction to Quranic Sciences* (London: ICAS, 2009), 280–81. The chronology of revelation is based on the research of scholars such as M. H. Ma'rifat (*al-Tamhīd fī 'ulūm al-Qur'ān* [Qum: Dār al-Ta'āruf lil-Maṭbū'āt, 2010]) and A. 'A. Zanjānī (*Tārīkh al-Qur'ān* [Cairo: Mu'assasat al-Hindawī li-l-Ta'līm wa-l-Thaqāfa, 2014]); see also 'A. R. al-Suyūṭī, *al-Itqān fī 'ulūm al-Qur'ān* (Medina: Markaz al-Dirāsāt al-Qur'āniyya, 2005), 1:168–69.

1.1 The Forms of *Ṣalāt*

The origin of the word *ṣalāt* is the Aramaic tri-literal root *ṣād-lām-alif*. In its original acceptation it meant to kneel down or bow (*raka'a*) and to bend over (*inḥinā*), but soon came to denote devotional prayer.[13] The Jews began to utilise the word in the Hebrew-Aramaic language, in which it was pronounced '*ṣalūta*'. In time, the word was also used by the Christians in the sense of prayer. Before Islam, the *ahl al-kitāb* (People of the Book)[14] introduced the word into the Arabic language.[15] The fact that the Qur'an uses the verb *ṣallā* in the initial revelations to the Prophet (96:10) implies that the word and concept was part of the language of the audience in Mecca. In Sūrat al-Anfāl, the Qur'an rejects the claim of the Arabs in Mecca that they were 'the guardians' of the sacred mosque (8:34), and then makes reference to their rituals with the Arabic '*ṣalātuhum*' ('their prayer'):

> Their prayer at the House [of God] is nothing but whistling and clapping of hands.[16] Therefore [its only answer can be]: 'taste the punishment, for you disbelieved.' (8:35)

The extension of *ṣalāt* as performed by the people of Mecca is stated in this verse. It demonstrates that the word *ṣalāt* was an established concept in the Arabic language and suggests that the Arabs believed their form of *ṣalāt* was meaningful and an appropriate way of communing with the Higher Power. The exegetes (*mufassirūn*) state that the Arabs of Mecca considered the acts of bowing (*al-rukū'*) and prostration (*al-sujūd*) as humiliating.[17] Hence, these were not included in their ritual devotions. Moreover, *ḥadīth* narrations corroborate the fact that prior to revelation the Arabs used to pray 'their *ṣalāt*'; they state that the Meccan Arabs used to perform prayers for their deceased prior to burial and at graves.[18] Thus, the word *ṣalāt* was understood by the Arabs in Mecca to mean 'connecting with a Higher Power through prayers, seeking forgiveness and supplicating'.

---

13 J. 'Alī, *Tārīkh al-ṣalāt fī al-Islām* (Baghdad: Maṭba'at Ḍiyā', 1968), 7.

14 The Qur'an employs this expression to refer collectively to the Jews and Christians.

15 'Alī, *Tārīkh al-ṣalāt*, 7.

16 According to the exegetes, 'the *ṣalāt* of the Quraysh of Mecca' ('*ṣalātuhum*') referred to their supplications. That is, they whistled and clapped their hands as a way of supplicating and glorifying God. See ibid., 9–11.

17 Ibid., 14.

18 Ibid., 11.

The first chapter to be revealed – Sūrat al-ʿAlaq – asks: 'Have you seen the one who prevents a servant [of God] from prayer?' (96:9–10). This verse was revealed in response to Abū Jahl ibn Hishām preventing the Prophet from praying.[19] It also marks the first instance of the verb *ṣallā*, or any of its derivatives, being mentioned in the revelation. This not only implies that the word and concept of *ṣalāt* existed in the Arabic language but more importantly that the Prophet was practising some form of *ṣalāt* before this verse was revealed. The exact form of this prayer is unknown; however, one may deduce that it included the actions of standing (*al-qiyām*), bowing and prostration for two reasons: first, the latter two actions were part of the prayer signified by the Hebrew-Aramaic word *ṣalūta*, which was being practised by both the Jews[20] and the monotheistic Arabs belonging to the tradition of the Prophet Ismāʿīl,[21] of which the Prophet would have been aware; and second, the actions of bowing and prostration were deemed as particularly reprehensible by the Arabs of Mecca, as mentioned above. The latter reason explains Abū Jahl's aversion to the Prophet's form of *ṣalāt*. Based on the Qur'an, *ḥadīth* literature and history, it seems that the Arabs of Mecca had only just begun to express their dislike for the Prophet's form of prayer; that is, there are no records of the Arabs expressing such opposition prior to revelation, which indicates that the Prophet's prayers may not have included the actions of bowing and prostration, assuming he prayed in public.

Thus, prior to revelation, the exact form of the Prophet's prayer, which includes what he recited, is unknown.[22] It is likely that it did not include the actions of bowing and prostration because, as mentioned above, the first record of opposition to the Prophet's form of *ṣalāt*, and indeed to his person, is once the revelations had begun. Hence, the Prophet was performing *ṣalāt* that included the actions of bowing and prostration very soon after the initial revelations; however, their number, order and what was recited are unknown.

The first command to establish *ṣalāt* is in Sūrat al-Muzzammil – the third chapter to be revealed in Mecca – wherein the Prophet is ordered to 'establish prayers for half of the night or slightly less' (73:2–4).[23] The command was issued

19 M. J. al-Ṭabarī, *Jāmiʿ al-bayān fī taʾwīl al-Qurʾān* (Beirut: Dār al-Kutub al-ʿIlmiyya, 2014), 12:647.

20 ʿAlī, *Tārīkh al-ṣalāt*, 12.

21 Qur'an 19:54–55.

22 ʿA. I. A. al-Ḥalabiyya, *al-Sīra al-Ḥalabiyya: Insān al-ʿūyūn fī al-Amīn al-Maʾmūn* (Beirut: Dār al-Kutub al-ʿIlmiyya, 2006), 1:381.

23 It should be noted that establishing prayers for lengthy periods of the night was a norm in both Judaism and Christianity prior to Islam (see Tanakh, Psalm 119:62), and the

within the first few years after the initial revelation.[24] The *ḥadīth* literature and books of history state that this practice continued for ten years;[25] whereupon, it was revoked by the last verse of Sūrat al-Muzzammil, which abrogates its performance.[26] However, this verse is Medinan, which was added to the *sūra* later in Medina. This is evinced by the fact that the verse also issues the command to pay *zakāt* and makes a reference to those who are 'fighting in the way of God'. These portions of the verse definitively situate its revelation in Medina, because the Muslims only began to fight in order to defend themselves and pay *zakāt* in Medina.[27] Furthermore, there are *ḥadīth*s stating that the verse was revealed in Medina in light of the fact that the Prophet was continuing the practice of praying throughout the night there.[28] Therefore, this practice was finally revoked in the initial years of the Prophet's migration to Medina.

Regarding the form of every *ṣalāt* performed during the night (*qiyām al-layl*), *ḥadīth* literature and works of history indicate that the Prophet was taught the form of *wuḍū'* (ablutions) and *ṣalāt* – that is, its actions and the fact that it consisted of two units (*rak'atān*) – by the angel Jibrā'īl soon after the revelations began.[29] Therefore, each *ṣalāt* performed during the night would have

Prophet was also practising it prior to the revelations, according to the *ḥadīth* literature (see 'A. M. S. Ibn Athīr, *al-Kāmil fī al-tārīkh* [Beirut: Dār al-Ṣādir, 1978], 2:48); hence, this Qur'anic exhortation was an instruction to the Prophet's followers to commence the performance of a norm that existed in other religions and was already being practised by the Prophet.

24 'Alī, *Tārīkh al-ṣalāt*, 25.

25 See 'A. R. al-Suyūṭī, *al-Durr al-manthūr fī al-tafsīr bi-l-ma'thūr* (Beirut: Dār al-Fikr, 1993), 8:312–13; and al-Ṭabarī, *Jāmi' al-bayān*, 12:279. Here, the *ḥadīth* literature also states that Sūrat al-Muzzammil was revealed over the course of one year; hence, there is a view that the norm of establishing *ṣalāt* for as much of the night as possible persisted for only a year, after which the final verse of Sūrat al-Muzzammil would have abrogated it. However, this cannot be the case since the final verse of Sūrat al-Muzzammil was revealed in Medina. See also M. Ḥ. al-Ṭabāṭabā'ī, *al-Mīzān fī tafsīr al-Qur'ān* (Beirut: Mu'assasat al-A'lamī li-l-Maṭbū'āt, 1997), 20:80–81.

26 Qur'an 73:20.

27 al-Ṭabāṭabā'ī, *al-Mīzān*, 20:80–81; 'Alī, *Tārīkh al-ṣalāt*, 25.

28 al-Ṭabarī, *Jāmi' al-bayān*, 12:279.

29 'A. M. Ibn Hishām, *al-Sīra al-nabawiyya* (Beirut: Dār wa-Maktabat al-Hilāl, 1998), 1:196. The *ḥadīth* literature and books of history state that after being taught by Jibrā'īl, the Prophet taught his wife Khadīja and his few followers. Other reports and historical records state that the Prophet would often pray with his wife Khadīja and his cousin 'Alī ibn Abī Ṭālib; the former died before the event of the Prophet's ascension (*al-mi'rāj*), which occurred prior to his migration to Medina. See Ibn Hishām, *al-Sīra al-nabawiyya*,

followed suit. As mentioned above, it is unknown as regards to the content of what was recited.[30] It is very probable that during the actions of bowing and prostration, the recitations would have comprised the praise (*taḥmīd*) and glorification (*tasbīḥ*) of God. However, during the postures of standing and sitting (*al-quʿūd*), not only are the recitations unknown, but they certainly would not have comprised the content of today's *ṣalāt* since very few *surās* had been revealed; for instance, Sūrat al-Fātiḥa (the fifth chapter to be revealed) was revealed several years after the first revelation to the Prophet.[31] In fact, it can be surmised that the content would have varied as and when more verses of the Qur'an were revealed.

Scholars state that the 'ten years' mentioned in the *ḥadīth* literature above, the duration of 'establishing prayers for a substantial period of every night', was superseded by the five daily prayers. The obligation to perform the five daily prayers was issued on the event of *al-isrā' wa-l-miʿrāj* (the night journey and ascension);[32] prior to this, no such obligation to perform *ṣalāt* per se was issued.[33] This suggests that the command to 'establish prayers for a substantial period of every night' in Sūrat al-Muzzammil was not an obligation in the jurisprudential sense. Scholars differ as to when the event of *al-isrā' wa-l-miʿrāj* occurred.[34] However, the majority of the scholars of *ḥadīth* place the event within the last twelve to eighteen months prior to the Prophet's migration to Medina.[35] Thus, the followers of the Prophet began to recite the five daily prayers after this event, where each *ṣalāt* consisted of only two units (*rakʿatān*).[36] This change in the form of *ṣalāt* was precipitated by the context of the Prophet agreeing to migrate to Medina after the city's Arab leaders had accepted his message on behalf of their tribesmen. Hence, the change in context seems to correspond with the change in the number and spiritual calibre of the followers of the

1:197.

30 al-Ḥalabiyya, *al-Sīra al-Ḥalabiyya*, 1:381.

31 ʿAlī, *Tārīkh al-ṣalāt*, 54.

32 The event of *al-isrā' wa-l-miʿrāj* is mentioned in the first verse of Sūrat al-Isrā', the fiftieth chapter to be revealed, and Sūrat al-Najm (53:1–18), the twenty-third chapter to be revealed.

33 al-Ḥalabiyya, *al-Sīra al-Ḥalabiyya*, 1:380.

34 M. R. M. Nor, 'Islamic Jerusalem: The Land of the Night Journey and Ascension', *Journal of Islamic Jerusalem Studies* 7 (2006): 7–9.

35 Ibid., 10.

36 ʿAlī, *Tārīkh al-ṣalāt*, 29. The increase in the units of the five daily prayers occurs within the first year after the Prophet's migration to Medina.

Prophet: prior to this change in the form of *ṣalāt*, the followers were few and devout; the sudden increase in his followers meant that the norm had to change from praying for a substantial period of every night to the five daily prayers, as the former would not have been sustainable for the spiritual growth of his followers in Medina; that is, the formulation of the essence must cater for the spiritual needs of the lowest common denominator.

The first revelation in Mecca that makes an explicit allusion to the obligatoriness of establishing prayers is found in Sūrat al-An'ām: '...and we are commanded to submit to the Lord of the Worlds, and to establish prayers ...' (6:71–72). The first revelation in Mecca that directly commands the Prophet and his followers to establish *ṣalāt* is in Sūrat al-Rūm: 'Turning to Him; and be mindful of Him and establish prayers, and be not of those who ascribe partners' (30:31). The direct command is repeated in Sūrat al-'Ankabūt: 'Recite that which has been revealed to you of the Book, and establish prayer ...' (29:45). Surās al-An'ām, al-Rūm and al-'Ankabūt are the fifty-fifth, eighty-fourth (antepenultimate) and eighty-fifth (penultimate) chapters to be revealed in Mecca, respectively. This tallies with the view of the majority of scholars that no obligation to perform *ṣalāt* was issued prior to the event of *al-isrā' wa-l-mi'rāj*, referred to in Sūrat al-Najm and Sūrat al-Isrā' – the twenty-third and fiftieth chapters to be revealed, respectively. There are approximately thirty-five verses in the Meccan chapters, including the aforementioned verses of Sūrat al-Rūm and Sūrat al-'Ankabūt, that utilise the verb *ṣallā* (to pray) and its nominal and verbal derivatives.[37] The vast majority do not signify the jurisprudential obligation to establish regular *ṣalāt*; collectively, they do express the inseparability of one's faith in God and establishing the norm of *ṣalāt*. There are four verses within the Meccan chapters that do utilise the imperative forms of the verb *aqāma* (to establish) in conjunction with *ṣalāt*, and one verse that uses the imperative *ṣallī* directly; however, none qualify as explicit prescriptions to establish *ṣalāt* in the jurisprudential sense.

In the period between the command 'to establish prayers for a substantial period of every night' in Sūrat al-Muzzammil and the issuance of the obligation to pray the five daily prayers on the night of *al-isrā' wa-l-mi'rāj*, the Prophet and his followers were reciting two prayers (*ṣalātān*) per day in Mecca, each consisting of two units: one at daybreak, which was known as *ṣalāt al-ḍuḥā*, and the other

37 See Qur'an 96:9–10, 73:20, 74:43, 87:15, 108:2, 75:31, 7:170, 35:18, 35:29, 19:31, 19:55, 19:59, 20:14, 20:132, 27:3, 17:78, 17:110, 10:87, 11:87, 11:114, 6:71–72, 6:92, 6:162, 31:17, 42:36, 42:38, 14:31, 14:37, 14:40, 21:73, 23:2, 23:9, 70:19–23, 70:34, 30:31, 29:45, 8:35.

in the afternoon, known as *ṣalāt al-ʿishā* or *ṣalāt al-ʿaṣr*.[38] This corresponds with the fact that eleven or so Meccan verses employing the word *ṣalāt* and its other verbal derivatives were revealed during the above interim, emphasising *ṣalāt* as a pivotal means of devotion to God.[39] Some scholars infer that the Prophet and his followers were reciting the *ṣalātān* in Mecca because of specific revealed instructions. They cite verse 114 of Sūrat al-Hūd (the fifty-second chapter to be revealed in Mecca), which issues the command to establish prayers at the ends of the day and at night (11:114); verse 78 of Sūrat al-Isrā' (the fiftieth chapter to be revealed), which issues the command to establish prayers at sunset until the dark of the night (17:78); and verse 130 of Surā Ṭāhā (the forty-fifth chapter to be revealed), which commands that God be glorified at daybreak and sunset (20:130). However, all of these verses were revealed in Medina.

Ibn Ḥajar al-Haytamī concisely summarises the chronological presentation thus far:

> Initially, the people had no responsibility other than to accept the message of 'the Oneness of God' (*al-tawḥīd*); this continued for a long period, until the command to establish *ṣalāt* during the night was revealed in Sūrat al-Muzzammil; this was subsequently abrogated by the prescription of the five daily prayers on the night of *al-isrā' wa-l-miʿrāj*; and no other obligations were issued until the Prophet migrated to Medina.[40]

In Medina, the Prophet increased the units of the five daily prayers within the first year of his arrival.[41] This is also evinced by the fact that the dispensation of shortening the five daily prayers was issued in Sūrat al-Nisā', the sixth chapter to be revealed in Medina: 'And when you travel in the land, there is no sin on you if you shorten your *ṣalāt*, if you fear that those who disbelieve may attack you...' (4:101). Similarly, the obligation to perform *wuḍū'* (ablutions) prior to the commencement of the *ṣalāt* was issued in verse six of Sūrat al-Mā'ida, the twenty-sixth chapter to be revealed in Medina; it is not mentioned in the Qur'an before this. Books of history and *ḥadīth* make reference to the event when Jibrā'īl

38 al-Ḥalabiyya, *al-Sīra al-Ḥalabiyya*, 1:376, 380.

39 The number eleven is based on the assumption that the event of *al-isrā' wa-l-miʿrāj* occurred around the time that Sūrat al-Isrā' was revealed (the fiftieth chapter to be revealed).

40 al-Ḥalabiyya, *al-Sīra al-Ḥalabiyya*, 1:376, 380–81.

41 M. J. al-Ṭabarī, *Tārīkh al-umam wa-l-mulūk* (Cairo: Maṭbaʿat al-Istiqāma, 1939), 2:119.

taught the Prophet the forms of *wuḍū'* and *ṣalāt*, and situate it in Mecca.[42] Scholars are divided as to whether the obligation to perform *wuḍū'* occurred in Mecca or Medina; all agree that it was taught to the Prophet in Mecca by Jibrā'īl as per the reports.[43] However, since the majority of scholars assert that there was no obligation to perform *ṣalāt* prior to the event of *al-isrā' wa-l-mi'rāj*, it is highly probable that the obligation to perform *wuḍū'* would have followed suit. The detailed timings of the five daily prayers and their stipulation as timed obligations are stated in Sūrat al-Baqara (2:238), Sūrat al-Nūr (24:58), Sūrat al-Hūd (11:114) and Sūrat al-Isrā' (17:78); that is, during the Medinan period. However, these verses would have been merely re-emphasising the times of worship established after the event of *al-isrā' wa-l-mi'rāj* that are alluded to in Sūrat al-Rūm, the eighty-fourth and antepenultimate chapter to be revealed in Mecca: 'So [give] glory to God when you enter the night and when you enter the morning ... and at the sun's decline [that is, afternoon] and at midday' (30:17–18).

The *ḥadīth* literature also states that the prohibition to answer others (or return their greetings) during *ṣalāt* was legislated a considerable while after the norm of performing *ṣalāt* was established in Mecca; indeed, talking to others about their needs during *ṣalāt* was considered something quite ordinary, and none of the Prophet's followers felt any hesitation in engaging in this until the prohibition was issued. Scholars differ as to whether this occurred before or after *hijra* due to differing *ḥadīths*. Some *ḥadīths* state that speaking during *ṣalāt* was permitted until the following verse of Sūrat al-Baqarā (the first chapter to be revealed in Medina) was issued: 'Pay constant attention to prayers and to the middle prayer, and stand truly obedient to Allah' (2:238). Others state that the Prophet would return greetings during prayers prior to his followers seeking asylum in Abyssinia, after which he prohibited any form of speaking during *ṣalāt*.[44] The former traditions situate the issuance of the prohibition in Medina, and the latter in Mecca.

---

42 Ibn Hishām, *al-Sīra al-nabawiyya*, 1:196.

43 The following are the opinions of the scholars as to when the obligation to perform *wuḍū'* was issued: (1) It was made obligatory in Mecca a year before the migration to Medina. (2) It became obligatory with the obligation of the five daily prayers on the night of *al-isrā' wa-l-mi'rāj*. (3) It was a 'recommended' (*mandūb*) duty before the night of *al-isrā' wa-l-mi'rāj*, and it became an obligatory act after this event. (4) It was a 'recommended' (*mandūb*) duty before the migration to Medina, and it became an obligatory act in Medina. See al-Ḥalabiyya, *al-Sīra al-Ḥalabiyya*, 1:377–79.

44 I. 'U. Ibn Kathīr, *Tafsīr al-Qur'ān al-'Aẓīm* (Beirut: Dār al-Andalus, 1996), 1:522–23; al-Ṭabarī, *Jāmi' al-bayān*, 2:584–87.

Sūrat al-Fātiḥa (1:1–7), the fifth chapter to be revealed in Mecca, is an intrinsic and essential component of the form of *ṣalāt* practised today, though obviously it could not have been part of the *ṣalāt* prior to its revelation. Scholars agree that it was revealed long after the initial revelations began; that is, between two and four years after the revelations began.[45] Therefore, during this period, Sūrat al-Fātiḥa would not have been part of the *ṣalāt*. Some scholars hold that it was revealed in Medina, and others state that it was revealed in both Mecca and Medina.[46] Based on *ḥadīth* literature, the majority opinion is that Jibrā'īl informed the Prophet of its mandatory recitation in every *ṣalāt* during the occasion when the *qibla* (direction of *ṣalāt*) was changed, which occurred in Medina.[47] This means that prior to this, the form of *ṣalāt* did not entail the mandatory recitation of Sūrat al-Fātiḥa in each of the first two units. The obligatory recitation of Sūrat al-Fātiḥa marks the completion of the form of *ṣalāt* in terms of the content that is recited in every unit; however, the content that is recited today was strictly defined by the different schools of *fiqh*.[48]

The Prophet also introduced the forms of *ṣalāt al-jumu'a* (the friday prayer),[49] *ṣalāt al-'īdayn* (the prayer of the two Eid days),[50] *ṣalāt al-janā'iz* (the funeral prayer)[51] and *ṣalāt al-khawf* (the prayer of fear)[52] in Medina, among others. These gradually evolved in their respective details. Although they are not connected to the five daily prayers, their introduction in Medina, in accordance with – and for the purpose of 'spiritualising' – the occasions and happenings of the community, further emphasises the interrelatedness and contingency of all regulations upon the context.

Finally, the Qur'an employs the word *ṣalāt* eighty-three times; fifty-four

45 This calculation is based on the fact that the revelation of Sūrat al-Muzzammil (the third chapter to be revealed) began within the first few years after the initial revelation and it took a year for all of its verses to be revealed.

46 Ibn Kathīr, *Tafsīr al-Qur'ān al-'Aẓīm*, 1:17–20.

47 'Alī, *Tārīkh al-ṣalāt*, 54. The changing of the qibla occurred during the second year after *hijra*. See al-Ṭabarī, *Tārīkh al-umam wa-l-mulūk*, 2:128–29.

48 M. J. Maghniyya, *The Five Schools of Islamic Law* (Qum: Ansariyan Publications, 2003), 89–99.

49 The Prophet first recited this when he entered Medina, after which the form gradually evolved. See al-Ṭabarī, *Tārīkh al-umam wa-l-mulūk*, 2:114–16.

50 *Ṣalāt al-'īd al-fiṭr* was introduced by the Prophet in the second year after the migration to Medina. See ibid., 2:129.

51 'Alī, *Tārīkh al-ṣalāt*, 71.

52 This was first introduced by the Prophet in the sixth year after the migration to Medina. See ibid., 73–74.

of which are found in the Medinan verses.[53] There are only eight instances in the Medinan verses when either the verbal derivatives of the verb *ṣallā* or the word *ṣalāt* are used in senses other than the formal Muslim practice of devotion that included the actions of bowing and prostration; that is, when their sentential utility provides the significations of blessings, supplications, prayers of non-human entities and synagogues. This, together with the aforementioned contextual deliberations on the forms of *ṣalāt*, suggests that the meaning of the word *ṣalāt* had changed during the Medinan period from its previous generic signification[54] (of 'supplication' and 'seeking forgiveness') to the 'Muslim' form of devotion that included the actions of bowing and prostration; that is, the transfer of the meaning of the word *ṣalāt* had occurred during the revelatory era (*al-ḥaqīqa al-shar'iyya*[55]). Of course, such a conclusion is unacceptable in *uṣūl al-fiqh*. This is because it assumes that only an atomistic reading of the words in the Qur'an can determine whether the associated meaning of a word in the minds of the people was established during the revelatory era or outside of it (*al-ḥaqīqa al-mutasharri'iyya*) – which is impossible in any case.[56] In conclusion, it is evident that every aspect of the form of *ṣalāt* gradually evolved

---

53 M. F. 'Abd al-Bāqī, *al-Mu'jam al-mufahras li-alfāẓ al-Qur'ān al-Karīm* (Cairo: Dār al-Ḥadīth, 2001), 507–509.

54 That is, among the Arabs; however, as mentioned above, for the *ahl al-kitāb*, the word *ṣalāt* would have had the additional signification of it being a devotional practice that included the actions of bowing and prostration.

55 This term refers to the fact that the transfer of the meaning of a word occurred during the revelatory era. Its antonym is *al-ḥaqīqa al-mutasharri'iyya*, which refers to the transfer of the meaning of a word outside of the revelatory era by the adherents of the Sharī'a. See M. R. Muẓaffar, *Uṣūl al-fiqh* (Qum: Intishārāt Ismā'īliyyāt, 2004), 1:37–39.

56 It is impossible because the meaning of a word in a text or speech is acquired in the mind of the reader or listener by sentential utility and not the spontaneous associated meanings of the words; that is, the other words in a sentence play the defining role in disclosing the exact meanings of the words of a sentence, rather than the spontaneous associated meanings of the words that exist in the mind of the reader or listener, which are of little significance in themselves in the sense-production of sentences in a text. (This is not to deny the necessity of the associated meanings of words, and their essential role, in the production of coherent and meaningful sentences in every language, or the fact that spontaneous associated meanings of the words exist.) Hence, a mere atomistic appreciation of a text will never be able to disclose the associated meaning of a word that exists in the minds of particular people at a particular time. Rather, the uncovering of the associated meaning of a word of a bygone people entails a holistic approach that includes both contextual investigations as well as in-depth analyses of texts, which include the atomistic appreciation of texts.

as the context of the Prophet changed and new issues arose. Perhaps the most significant contextual factor in its evolution is the fact that the followers of the Prophet increased, and hence, their spiritual calibre became more varied. Consequently, it became increasingly formalised in the Medinan context of a community of believers living alongside other religious communities.

The following is a summary of the findings of this section: (1) In Mecca, the verbal content of the *ṣalāt* was not specified at all and was left to the discretion of the reciter. (2) The timings of *ṣalāt* were not stipulated in Mecca until the command was issued in Sūrat al-Muzzammil to establish *ṣalāt* for a substantial period of every night. From this point onwards (or perhaps even before it) until the event of *al-isrāʾ wa-l-miʿrāj*, the Prophet and his followers were also reciting *ṣalāt* twice a day in the morning and afternoon. After the event, the five daily prayers were instated, and were understood by his followers to be mandatory. (3) Prior to the event of *al-isrāʾ wa-l-miʿrāj*, the obligatoriness of *ṣalāt* (and *wuḍūʾ*) was never expressed, as the need had not arisen. The few followers of the Prophet were very devoted to God and would not have needed prompting to pray. Indeed, they were establishing prayers throughout the night, every night. However, just prior to the event, the leaders of the tribe of Khazraj became his followers and invited the Prophet to Medina in order to arbitrate and resolve their conflicts with the tribe of Aws. Thereafter, the obligation to perform the five daily prayers was explicitly issued on the night of *al-isrāʾ wa-l-miʿrāj* in light of the fact that all of the members of the tribes of Aws and Khazraj had become his followers. (4) Throughout Mecca, each *ṣalāt* consisted of two units (*rakʿatān*) only; this was also the case for the five daily prayers when they were first instated. It is only in Medina that the units for four of the five daily prayers were increased. (5) Sūrat al-Fātiḥa became a mandatory part of every *ṣalāt* in Medina when the Prophet was instructed to change the direction (*qibla*) of *ṣalāt* to Mecca. (6) The forms of *ṣalāt* in Mecca gradually evolved to become the five daily prayers. In Medina, other forms of *ṣalāt* were gradually introduced in the context of the happenings and occasions of the community of believers.

1.2 The Forms of Zakāt

The origin of the word *zakāt* follows the same trajectory as that of *ṣalāt* mentioned above. In Sumerian and the ancient Semitic languages, the derivatives of the root letters *z-k-w* have the meaning of 'purity' and 'exemption from the payment of taxes'. The latter was the predominant meaning of the word *zakūta*, whose origin is Sumerian.[57] The words *zakūta* and *ṣidakta* are found in Aramaic, and *ṣidaka* in Hebrew.[58] They usually signified 'purity' and were utilised by the Jews and Christians in the context of virtuous conduct; however, *ṣidakta* was also used in Aramaic to signify alms.[59] The derivatives of the root *z-k-h* are utilised in the Bible with the meanings of being vindicated, clean and morally clean.[60] As was the case with the Arabic word *ṣalāt*, the origin of the Arabic word *zakāt* is the Aramaic-Hebrew language that was spoken by the Jews and Christians.

In the chronological examination of the utility of the verb *zakā* and its derivatives in the Meccan verses of the Qur'an, the first verse is in Sūrat al-Aʿlā, the eighth chapter to be revealed, in which the verb *tazakkā* is utilised to mean 'he has been purified' (87:14). In fact, until Sūrat al-Aʿrāf, the thirty-ninth chapter to be revealed, the verbs *tazakkā*, *yatazakkā*, *tuzakkū*, *yazzakkā* and *zakkā* are each employed only once in the sense of self-purification and growth. Of these, it is only the verb *yatazakkā* in Sūrat al-Layl, the ninth chapter to be revealed, that it is employed in the sense of self-purification resulting from giving of one's wealth (92:18). The word *zakāt* is first utilised in Sūrat al-Aʿrāf in the sense of 'alms' (7:156). God replies to the Prophet Mūsā's supplication in which He describes those who are worthy of His salvation as 'those who are mindful [of God] and give the *zakāt*' (7:156). Here, *zakāt* is used for the first time in the sense of 'giving of wealth in the way of God'. Prior to this, the revelations did not employ the verb *zakā* and its derivatives to signify 'alms' or 'alms-giving'; rather, four verses were revealed highlighting the attitude of the Meccan people towards the poor, criticising their suboptimal practices of alms-giving and mentioning the categories of those in need.[61]

57 S. Bashear, 'On the Origins and Development of the Meaning of *Zakāt* in Early Islam', *Arabica* 40, no. 1 (1993): 87.

58 The origin of the Qur'anic notion of *ṣadaqa*.

59 C. C. Torrey, *The Jewish Foundation of Islam* (New York: Jewish Institute of Religion Press, 1933), 141.

60 Bashear, 'On the Origins and Development of the Meaning of *Zakāt* in Early Islam', 89.

61 The first reference to the poor (*miskīn*) among the Arabs of Mecca is in Sūrat al-Qalam, the second chapter to be revealed, which conveys the attitude of indifference among the farmers towards the poor and their reluctance to assist them (68:24). The second is in Sūrat al-Muddaththir, the fourth chapter to be revealed, in which the inhabitants of hell state that the cause of their burning is their refusal to feed the poor (74:44). Both of these verses were revealed some years prior to the first utility of a derivative of the verb *zakā* in the Qur'an, which was *tazakkā* in Sūrat al-Aʿlā. The third reference is in Sūrat al-Najm, the twenty-third chapter to be revealed, in which the Meccan norm of alms-giving is referred to; it criticises the Meccan people for the meagre amounts they

After Sūrat al-Aʿrāf, the next revelation to utilise the derivatives of the verb *zakā* is found in Sūrat al-Fāṭir, the forty-third chapter to be revealed; the verse employs the verbs *tazakkā* and *yatazakkā*, and marks the first time that the word *ṣalāt* and the derivatives of the verb *zakā* appear together in the revelations: 'You can only warn those who fear their Lord in secret, and establish the *ṣalāt*; and whoever gives *zakāt*, he only purifies his own self' (35:18). It should be noted that the phrase '*man tazakkā*' in this verse is commonly translated as 'whoever is purified'. In the same chapter, there is another verse that refers to those who establish *ṣalāt* and spend of their wealth in charity; however, the latter is not referred to by the derivatives of the verb *zakā*: 'Those who recite the Book of Allah and establish the *ṣalāt* and spend of what We have granted them as sustenance secretly and openly, hope for a trade-gain that will never perish' (35:29).

In the Meccan verses, the derivatives of the root *zakā* are employed twenty-three times: fourteen derivatives are connected with the sense of purity and growth, which include two uses of the word *zakāt* signifying 'purity'; the remaining nine instances are the word *zakāt* signifying 'alms', and as mentioned above the word *zakāt* is employed from Sūrat al-Aʿrāf onwards. The nine verses employing the word *zakāt* in the sense of 'alms' do not convey any sense of performative obligation: seven describe the faithful as those who establish prayers and give *zakāt* as a means to purifying the soul; one describes those who ascribe partners to God (*mushrikīn*) as those who do not give *zakāt*; and one contrasts the consequences of giving *zakāt* with those of giving out usury. Thus, it can be surmised that during the Meccan period, whenever the word *zakāt* was accompanied by the verb *atā*, the signification was alms-giving for the sake of God without any sense of obligation.

The chronological reading of the Medinan verses of the Qur'an reveals a striking difference in the usage of the verb *zakā* and its derivatives when compared to their utility in the Meccan verses above. All eleven verbal derivatives are used to emphasise either that God is the sole agent of purification in humans or that it is the Prophet's role to purify the people. Employment of the verbal derivatives in the sense of 'purifying oneself' is totally absent, which constituted the main sense of their usage in the Meccan verses. Undoubtedly, this shift in emphasis on who bears the onus of purifying the soul – from being exclusively upon 'oneself'

---

give as alms and for being miserly (53:34). The fourth reference is in Sūrat al-Balad, the thirty-fifth chapter to be revealed, which lists the different types of poor and needy persons in Meccan society (90:14).

in Mecca to being exclusively upon 'God and His Prophet' in Medina – is due to the change in context and audience; the lowest common denominator in terms of spiritual calibre among the Prophet's followers in Mecca was extremely high in comparison to those in Medina. Of the twenty-three nominal derivatives employed, three occur in the form of the comparative adjective *azkā*, meaning 'purer', and the remainder in the meaning 'alms or wealth'. Eight instances of *zakāt* are accompanied by the imperative verb, signifying obligation: four of which are addressed to the Muslims; one to the wives of the Prophet; two to the Jews of Medina;[62] and one in the context of a covenant between God and the Jews. Nine instances of *zakāt* are utilised as part of the descriptions of various groups of people (mainly those who believe), two instances are employed as part of conditional sentences and one is used in the context of stating a historical covenant between God and the children of Isrā'īl.

Therefore, it can be surmised that in the Meccan verses the verb *zakā* and its derivatives were utilised to signify 'purification of oneself for the sake of God' generally until Sūrat al-A'rāf. Thereafter, the word *zakāt* began to be employed twice to signify 'purity' and nine times to signify 'alms'. The usage of the word *zakāt* in the latter sense had the connotation of 'the giving of wealth or alms to the needy in the way of God' without the sense of obligation. In the Medinan verses, the verbal derivatives of the verb *zakā* were utilised exclusively to emphasise that only God and the Prophet were the agent and means of purification, respectively. The most utilised derivative of the verb *zakā* is the word *zakāt*. It is employed a total of twenty times and its signification every time is the mandatory 'poor-rate tax', which constitutes a change in its form. This is more than double the number of times it was employed in the Meccan chapters, and its signification is no longer the charity-based 'alms' that it signified in the Meccan verses. This is because in eight of the Medinan verses, it is accompanied

62 See Qur'an 2:43 and 2:83. Early exegetes state that the commands to establish *ṣalāt* and pay *zakāt* in these verses were exhortations to the Jews of Medina to pray *ṣalāt* with the Prophet and his followers, and to give the latter their *zakāt*. See M. 'U. al-Zamakhsharī, *al-Kashshāf* (Beirut: Dār Iḥyā' al-Turāth al-'Arabī, 2001), 1:161; M. Ḥ. al-Ṭūsī, *al-Tibyān fī tafsīr al-Qur'ān* (Qum: Mu'assasat al-Nashr al-Islāmī, 1996), 2:156–58; 'A. A. al-Nasafī, *Madārik al-tanzīl wa-ḥaqā'iq al-ta'wīl* (Beirut: Dār al-Kutub al-'Ilmiyya, 2014), 1:47; F. H. al-Ṭabarsī, *Majma' al-bayān fī tafsīr al-Qur'ān* (Beirut: Mu'assasat al-A'lamī li-l-Maṭbū'āt, 1995), 1:189–90, 286; and Bashear, 'On the Origins and Development of the Meaning of *Zakāt* in Early Islam', 89–91. The implication here is that the Jews were being exhorted to recite the *ṣalāt* without the necessity of formally converting to the religion of the Prophet.

by the imperative verb, which signifies obligation. This difference in the tone and emphasis of *zakāt* in the Meccan and Medinan verses is indicative of the difference in the Prophet's role, context and audience. In Medina, he is the leader of both the Muslim and non-Muslim communities.[63] Hence, in the context of leadership of a diverse community the word *zakāt* is reformulated to signify 'a mandatory poor-rate tax to purify oneself and cater for the needs of society'. This institutionalised form of *zakāt* gradually developed in accordance with the structural growth of the Medinan society to cater for societal needs as they emerged. Hence, it would have increased in specificity over time, culminating in the designation of the types of people that qualified as recipients for *zakāt*; they are stated in Sūrat al-Tawba (9:60), the 130th chapter to be revealed, as being the poor, the needy, those employed in the administration of funds, those whose hearts may be won over to Islam, those in bondage and debt, the cause of Allah and the wayfarer.

It must be emphasised that the Qur'anic exhortation to pay *zakāt* is more than merely an obligation to pay taxes; it must be an action that is performed out of love for God and care towards one another. It seems that the Muslim community of Medina were less heedful of the latter condition; hence, the following verse was revealed to emphasise the importance of its inclusion in the performance of *zakāt*:

> It is not righteousness that you turn your faces towards the East and the West, but righteous is the one who believes in Allah, and the Last Day, and the angels and the Book and the prophets, and gives away wealth out of love for Him to the near of kin, the orphans, the needy, the wayfarer, to those who ask and to set slaves free, and establishes the *ṣalāt* and pays the *zakat.* (2:177)

During the Medinan period in which the society continued to grow and become more affluent, the notion of '*zakāt* on wealth' seems to have taken on the connotation of 'filth', as noted in certain narrations.[64] This explains the

63 E. Schaeublin, 'Zakat Practice in the Islamic Tradition and Its Recent History in the Context of Palestine', in *Histories of Humanitarian Action in the Middle East and North Africa*, ed. E. Davey and E. Svoboda (London: Overseas Development Institute, 2014), 20.

64 See Ḥ. al-ʿĀmalī, *Tafṣīl wasāʾil al-Shīʿa* (Qum: Muʾassasat Āl al-Bayt li-Iḥyāʾ al-Turāth, 1990), 9:268.

narrations in the *ḥadīth* literature that forbid the Prophet and his family from accepting *ṣadaqa* – i.e. charity that was not formally prescribed.[65] The reasoning could be that since the Prophet and his household enjoyed a special status (due to their being purified of all filth[66]), this would have prevented them from accepting anything deemed to be impure by the convention of that time, which would have included *zakāt*; the implication, here, is that if the convention did not deem *zakāt* as 'filth' or 'impurity' they would have been permitted to accept it. In any case, this restriction to accept or receive *zakāt* was extended by the community to include the family outside of the immediate household and descendants of the Prophet. In time, however, the descendants (*sādāt*) of the Prophet were permitted 'to consume' the *zakāt* of other *sādāt*; that is, they were permitted to consume one another's 'filth' but not of others.[67] Therefore, in principle, should *zakāt* lose its negative connotation of 'filth', or, in other words, should the convention of the people no longer deem *zakāt* as 'filth', then *zakāt* could be received by both *sayyid*s (descendants of the Prophet) and non-*sayyid*s.

The Qur'an refers to two other 'forms' of *zakāt*. These were nominally different taxes on wealth that nevertheless were also instituted on the basis of the needs and demands of the growing community, and which were to be performed for the sake of God in order to purify oneself; that is, they shared the same essence as *zakāt*. The first is a *khums* (fifth) on the spoils of war, which is mentioned in Sūrat al-Anfāl: 'And know that whatever thing you gain [as spoils of war], a fifth of it is for Allah and for the messenger and for the near of kin and the orphans and the needy and the wayfarer' (8:41). The other is *fay'*, spoils gained outside of the context of war, which is mentioned in Sūrat al-Ḥashr: 'That which Allah gives [as spoils] to his messenger from the people of the townships, it is for Allah and for the messenger and for the near of kin and the orphans and the needy and the wayfarer so that it may not alternate [as possessions] among the rich of you' (59:7). It will be noted that the recipients of both *khums* and *fay'* are identical; in fact, the last three are also eligible to receive *zakāt* as well. Ayatollah Khomeini gestures to the fact that the Qur'an's designation of specific categories of the needy as recipients of *zakāt* is contingent upon the existential needs of the growing community; hence, he increases

65 Ibid., 9:268–71; cf. A. Q. al-Khū'ī, *al-Mustanad fī sharḥ al-'Urwa al-wuthqā: Kitāb al-khums* (Qum: al-Maṭba'a al-'Ilmiyya, 2016), 198.

66 Qur'an 33:33.

67 See al-'Āmalī, *Tafṣīl wasā'il al-Shī'a*, 9:273–76.

the scope of the designation '*sabīl li-llāh*' (that is, giving in 'the way of God') to include all public benefits (*maṣāliḥ al-ʿāmma*).[68] Naturally, this is also true for both the stipulation of *khums* and *fay'* and the designation of their recipients. In addition to the existential needs of the community, the verse of *fay'* provides a further rationale, or principle, for all three taxes: that wealth should not remain among the wealthy; rather, it is to be distributed across society.

Regarding *khums*, it will be noted that the Qur'an makes no reference to the "*sayyid*/non-*sayyid*" distinction with regards to the orphans, needy and wayfarer; the criterion of *sayyid* was introduced and applied to these categories of the needy by the Imāms due to their context, which in all probability was because the needy among the *sayyids* were not receiving *zakāt* due to the prevalent belief that they could not consume it.[69] According to the *ḥadīth* literature, changes in context have also precipitated the following modifications to the regulation of *khums*: (1) Imām ʿAlī is reported to have forgone his share, and by implication was stating that the people pay the other half of *khums* (that is, to the orphans, needy and wayfarer).[70] (2) The fifth Imām added gold and silver coins to the list of items subject to *khums* in spite of their being subject to *zakāt*; when asked for the rationale, he is reported to have stated that it was necessary for a year in order to cater for the needs of the community,[71] and that he would forgo his share.[72] (3) The seventh and ninth Imāms extended the remit of *khums* to any surplus of every form of wealth.[73] (4) The twelfth Imām is reported to have permitted his followers to consume *khums*.[74] Such modifications are indicative of the contingency of the regulative forms of *khums* upon context and societal needs; thus, it shares the same essence as *zakāt*.

According to Ayatollah Khomeini and Ayatollah Muntazeri, *khums* was under-

68 See R. al-Khumaynī, *al-ʿUrwa al-wuthqā maʿa taʿālīq al-Imām al-Khumaynī* (Qum: Mu'assasat Tanẓīm wa-Nashr Āthār al-Imām al-Khumaynī, 2001), 629–30. Obviously, the category of 'societal needs' is subsumed under the designation of 'all public benefits' (*maṣāliḥ al-ʿāmma*). Moreover, 'public benefits' fluctuate as the context changes.

69 See al-ʿĀmalī, *Tafṣīl wasā'il al-Shīʿa*, 9:268–76, 483, and al-Ṭabarī, *Jāmiʿ al-bayān*, 6:251–52.

70 See narrations in ibid., 9:543, 547, 550.

71 al-Khū'ī, *al-Mustanad*, 200–203.

72 See al-ʿĀmalī, *Tafṣīl wasā'il al-Shīʿa*, 9:546.

73 al-Khū'ī, *al-Mustanad*, 199, 207. Ayatollah Khū'ī states that there is insufficient evidence for the application of khums on any form of surplus during the life of the Prophet. See ibid., 197–98.

74 See al-ʿĀmalī, *Tafṣīl wasā'il al-Shīʿa*, 9:550.

stood to be the possession of the institution of the head of state.[75] This seems justified in light of the fact that its origin was a practice in pre-Islamic Arabia in which the Arab chiefs would take a quarter of the spoils of war.[76] However, it must be emphasised that the stipulations of the various regulative forms of *khums* were in response to types of societal need. This is substantiated by the fact that the Imāms had no qualms in extending the remit of *khums* to all forms of savings in order to cater for the needs of their respective existential contexts.[77]

In conclusion, the Meccan verses of the Qur'an employ the verb *zakā* and its verbal derivatives in the sense of 'being pure', 'being purified' and 'purifying'. They put the onus of purification upon each individual; that is, one must endeavour to remove all defects from one's self by whatever means necessary: fostering a proper and wholesome attitude; caring for others; ridding oneself of associating partners with God (*shirk*), greed and disbelief (*kufr*); or giving of wealth. The word *zakāt* is employed a total of eleven times in the Meccan verses after the thirty-eighth chapter; nine of them are in sense of 'alms-giving in the way God'. In the Medinan verses, there is a change in both the utility of the verbal derivatives of the verb *zakā* and the signification of the word *zakāt*. The verbal derivatives are employed to signify that only God and his Prophet are the cause and means of purification, respectively; hence, the onus is on God and the Prophet to purify the individual, and the onus of the latter is exclusively to follow the Prophet. As mentioned above, this change in onus reflects the spiritual needs of the lowest common denominator among the followers of the Prophet in Medina. Similarly, all twenty usages of the word *zakāt* in the Medinan verses signify 'the mandatory poor-rate tax that is to be given in the way of God'. This, in light of the aforementioned contextual deliberations on the forms of *zakāt*, suggests that the meaning of the word *zakāt* had changed during the Medinan period from its previous generic signification of 'voluntary alms-giving in the way of God' to 'the mandatory poor-rate tax that is to be given in the way of God'.[78] This change in the signification of the word *zakāt* is

75 See 'A. A. S. al-Māzandarānī, *Dalīl taḥrīr al-wasīla – al-khums – al-Imām al-Khumaynī* (Tehran: Maṭba'at Mu'assasat al-'Urūj, 1996), 14–15; and Ḥ. 'A. Muntaẓarī, *Kitāb al-khums* (Qum: Dār al-Fikr, 1992), 11–13. The same point is made by A. Sachedina, 'Al-Khums: The Fifth in the Imāmī Shī'ī Legal System', *Journal of Near Eastern Studies* 39, no. 4 (1980): 286.

76 W. M. Watt, *Muhammad at Medina* (Oxford: Clarendon Press, 1956), 255.

77 Calder, 'Khums in Imāmī Shī'ī Jurisprudence', 39; Sachedina, 'Al-Khums', 283–86.

78 As previously mentioned, such a conclusion is unacceptable in *uṣūl al-fiqh*. This is because it assumes that only an atomistic reading of the words in the Qur'an can determine

due to the context of Medina, wherein the Prophet's role, his community and its societal needs differed significantly to his role in the community of Mecca.

2. Analysis of the Forms and Essences of *Ṣalāt* and *Zakāt* in the Qur'an

The chronological presentation of the Qur'anic verses, supplemented by the *ḥadīth* literature, reveals that *ṣalāt* gradually evolved. Throughout its evolution it remained as a fundamental spiritual practice congruent with the needs and progression of the Muslim community in order to facilitate its growth. It gradually developed from a generic voluntary act, appropriate for the nascent and few devoted followers of the Prophet in Mecca, to a detailed spiritual obligation, appropriate for the spiritual needs of the lowest common denominator in the Medinan community.[79] These modifications are tantamount to formal changes that were necessary in order to safeguard the spiritual essence of *ṣalāt*: to provide individuals with a specified period of intense God-centric orientation and, in turn, facilitate the emergence of a God-centric community and its subsequent subsistence (as a God-centric community) during its evolving existential state. It must be emphasised that its formal evolution came to an end in the Medinan period; that is, its form was now perfect and optimal for the spiritual growth of every Muslim.

Zakāt similarly underwent formal modifications in order to safeguard its spiritual essence: the purification of the individual from vices and moral inadequacies, the alleviation of poverty and the accommodation of societal needs. It was gradually ratified as a societal tax in Medina where the Prophet stipulated its details in accordance with the evolving existential context.[80] The chronological reading of the Qur'anic verses and supplementary *ḥadīth* literature above reveals the gradual evolution of its form from a voluntarily spiritual obligation of charity in the latter half of the Meccan period to a instituted form of tax on capital assets and wealth in the form of agricultural goods, livestock and other items that were considered wealth in the Medinan period.[81] Throughout the

---

whether the associated meaning of a word in the minds of the people was established during the revelatory era or outside of it (*al-ḥaqīqa al-mutasharriʿiyya*) – which is impossible in any case.

79 K. Mohammed, 'The Foundation of Muslim Prayer', *Medieval Encounters* 5, no. 1 (1999): 23.

80 J. Schacht, '*Zakāt*', in *Encyclopaedia of Islam* (Leiden: E. J. Brill, 1993), 4:1202–4.

81 R. Powell, 'Zakat: Drawing Insights for Legal Theory and Economic Policy from Islamic Jurisprudence', *Pitt. Tax Rev.* 7 (2009): 48.

Meccan period, the act of giving *zakāt* was understood as an act of charity that rids the heart of greed, which is a form of filth. This connotation continued in Medina in spite of its modification from its 'voluntary alms-giving' status to 'mandatory poor-rate tax'. The basis of the act of giving *zakāt* is the Qur'anic dictum of God being the exclusive and real owner (*mālik*) of the universe and everything in it, which means that everything that humans possess is God's bestowals upon them.[82] Hence, al-Ghazālī states that 'the bodily acts of worship are man's gratitude for the bodily blessings which God has bestowed upon him, while the financial acts of worship are his gratitude for financial gifts'.[83] Here, al-Ghazālī is emphasising the fact that *zakāt* is primarily a mode of worship and devotion to God; that is, it must be accompanied with the intention 'for the sake of God'.[84] This would have the effect of transmuting the merely outward action of giving wealth into an action of ablution or purification of the soul and its possessions just as *ṣalāt* purifies the soul and its body.[85] Therefore, giving charitable donations in general (*ṣadaqāt*), which includes *zakāt* in its formal sense, is a means to purifying both one's self and wealth, whereby the latter is worthy of consumption.[86] The other taxes discussed in the previous section are *khums* and *fay'*, both of which are essentially extensions of *zakāt*.[87] This is because 'societal need' is the impetus for both the initial stipulations of these taxes and their subsequent modifications.

This paper has demonstrated that in spite of *ṣalāt* being a spiritual obligation that was instated for the purpose of exclusively addressing the spiritual needs of the individual and community, it still underwent formal modifications in order to be optimal for the growth of both. This paper has also delineated that *zakāt*

82 W. B. Hallaq, *Sharia: Theory, Practice, Transformations* (Cambridge: Cambridge University Press, 2009), 296.

83 A. Ḥ. M. al-Ghazālī, *Iḥyā' 'ulūm al-dīn* (Beirut: Dār Ibn Ḥazm, 2005), 254.

84 Intention is an intrinsic part of the performance of *zakāt* because the essence of *zakāt* is 'the acquisition of inner purity by giving in the way of God'. To this effect, Imām 'Alī is attributed as having exhorted people not to invalidate their *zakāt* by failing to intend it for the sake of Allah. See 'A. Abī Ṭālib, *Nahj al-balāgha*, ed. Ṣ. al-Ṣāliḥ (Qum: Dār al-Ḥadīth li-l-Ṭabā'a wa-Nashr, 2005), 478 (sermon 199, section 'al-Zakāt'). This indicates that although the mere action of paying *zakāt* without the intention will contribute to the fulfilment of societal need, it is deficient from the spiritual perspective; its aspect of inner purification will not be achieved because it was being given without the appropriate intention.

85 Hallaq, *Sharia*, 231.

86 Powell, 'Zakat', 49.

87 Sachedina, 'Al-Khums', 276–77.

has always been a social obligation that was instated for purpose of addressing the societal needs of the community. It also underwent formal modifications in accordance with the needs of its differing contexts. Therefore, since the spiritual obligation of *ṣalāt*, which is considered by all as sacrosanct and eternal, was modified in accordance with the differing contexts, then by priority the social obligation of *zakat*, which is predicated upon societal need in any case, must be subject to ongoing and periodic modification so that it continues to fulfil its purpose (that is, its essence or function) of catering for the societal needs of the context.

CONCLUSION

The immutable part of *zakāt* is its essence: the purification of the soul by giving wealth for the sake of God to alleviate poverty and cater for societal needs. In contrast to this, the form of *zakāt* must fluctuate in accordance with differing existential contexts in order to fulfil its essence or function. Therefore, insofar as modern state taxes endeavour to redress poverty and cater for societal needs, they qualify as instances of *zakāt* as long as the taxpayer pays such taxes with the intention of 'for the sake of God'.[88]

In the previously mentioned verse of Sūrat al-Baqara, the Qur'an exhorts the mandatory establishing of *ṣalāt* and paying of *zakāt* in addition to the voluntary giving of '... wealth out of love for Him to the near of kin, the orphans, the needy, the wayfarer, to those who ask and to set slaves free . . .' (2:177). The recipients of both the mandatory *zakāt* and voluntary 'giving' are almost identical. The only reason for this exhortation to 'give' in addition to *zakāt* is because *zakāt* in itself was insufficient in alleviating poverty and catering for societal needs; hence, people were exhorted to give more. In reality, both are extensions of *zakat*, the difference being that one was state instituted and the other voluntary.[89] The Qur'an employs many other terms to stress the necessity and importance of 'giving more', such as *infāq* (spending God-consciously), *īthār* (preferring the other) and *ītā' al-māl* (giving of wealth).[90] This means that the spiritual obligation to voluntarily give *zakāt* continues beyond the

88 Calder, '*Zakāt* in Imāmī Shī'ī Jurisprudence', 473.

89 al-Ṭabāṭabā'ī, *al-Mīzān*, 1:429.

90 See Qur'an 2:177, 261–62, 264, 271, for examples of the utility of the word *infāq* and its derivatives; 59:9 for an example of the word *īthār*; and 2:277 for an example of the expression *ītā' al-māl*.

state-imposed taxation, should societal need and poverty subsist.

Since the words *ṣalāt* and *zakāt* frequently appear in the Qur'an together, this paper has analysed the evolution of the forms of both. It has been demonstrated that the forms of both have evolved in accordance with the changing context to optimise the intellectual, moral and spiritual growth of the individual and community. A pressing question may occur at this juncture: can the essence of *ṣalāt* be accommodated by other forms as is clearly the case with *zakāt*? It is important to address this question because the evolution of the voluntary form of *ṣalāt* into its obligatory form mirrors the evolution of the voluntary form of *zakāt* into its mandatory form. The former's change in status from a 'voluntary' act of devotion to its 'obligatory' status was also a response to a change in context; in Medina, the spiritual needs of the people would not have been adequately catered for by the former prescription to 'establish prayers for as much of the night as possible'. Therefore, can the form of *ṣalāt* undergo further change to optimise the spiritual growth of the people and community? The answer is a categorical 'no' because the Prophet's formulation of the final form of *ṣalāt* was designed to specifically and universally cater for the spiritual needs of the lowest common denominator in society. Furthermore, this paper has demonstrated through an etymological analysis of the word *ṣalāt* that the actions of bowing and prostration have always been intrinsic elements of the form of *ṣalāt*; hence, only radical changes in the existential context could warrant their 'formal' modification.[91] In contrast to this, *zakāt* is necessarily contingent upon the immediate needs of the societal context which, by its very nature, is perpetually fluctuating. To conclude, insofar as state taxes in the modern era are formulated in light of societal needs, then they do count as legitimate instances of *zakāt*. This is because the essence of *zakāt* is to cater for societal needs as they arise in human societies in order to facilitate the intellectual, moral and spiritual growth of the individual and community.

91 The contexts of space travel, the International Space Station, the moon and inhabiting other worlds would inevitably entail 'formal' modifications of *ṣalāt* in terms of changes to postures, timings and direction.

AHMED SAAD AL-AZHARI AL-HASANI

Prophetic Initiatives to Institutionalise Money Matters: An Historical Overview through al-Kittāni's *al-Tarātīb al-idāriyya*

Despite the copious literature dealing with pre-Islamic Arabs, many questions regarding the intricacies of their social and financial networks remain unanswered. Money matters, especially wealth distribution and charitable activities, remain even more ambiguous and in need of further exploration. One point regarding this area can, however, be confirmed: that Arabs cherished generosity and helped those in distress. Whether settled populations, nomads or semi-nomads, Arabs offered food to the hungry, clothes to the needy and would not leave the widows without support. They took pride in generosity as individuals as well as tribes. Regardless of the motivations of these charitable moves, they were generally spontaneous and unplanned, limited to the occasion of distress and not forward thinking, in addition to being mainly singular activities that lacked organisation and collective planning.

When the Prophet Muḥammad established what became known as the first civic society or city-state in Medina, his focus was to invest the good qualities of Arabs and put them in the right direction. Islamic injunctions of *zakāt*, charity and money-giving encouraged and fostered the Arabs' sense of generosity and was in line with their love for help. However, the biggest Islamic contribution was the systemisation of these activities. This happened at two levels: the moral, through encouraging the observation of balance in spending and avoidance of being stingy or a spendthrift; and the institutionalisation of money matters – nominating their beneficiary categories through revelation (deciding who can benefit from each fund) and centralising the process of deciding their amounts, collection, recording and distribution.

Sayyid ʿAbd al-Ḥayy ibn ʿAbd al-Kabīr al-Kittānī (d. 1962) detailed in his magnum opus *al-Tarātīb al-idāriyya* [The administrative organisation] the process of *zakāt*, tax, land revenue and charity collection introduced by the Prophet Muḥammad, what positions were introduced for the collection, distribution and recording of *zakāt* funds and what mechanisms of central and regional supervision and book-keeping were available. These forward-thinking activities are much needed in a Muslim minority context since the Medinan society is very similar to the context of European Muslims, who have the freedom to practise their faith as a minority. This paper looks at the details of this Prophetic activity and its merits and ability to inspire the current context. It further asks questions about, and sheds light on, an aspect of the Medinan society that is rarely discussed.

1. Pre-Islamic Charity and Money Matters

The copious literary sources dealing with pre-Islamic Arabian society do not, in general, provide enough detail about the actual running of Arabs' day-to-day lives, business arrangements and wealth distribution, but rather contain scant historical anecdotes limited to hyperbolic poetry and mythological stories.[1] From scarce lines of poetry that refer to a tribal leader's shares in public wealth incurred in warfare, we have an indication of not just the names they used in reference to different shares of common wealth, but the sizeable amount of public wealth dedicated to people in leading positions. In lamentation of the leader of Banu Shaybān, the pre-Islamic poet 'Abd Allāh ibn 'Anama said: 'To you belonged, one fourth of the booty and whatever else you choose. Besides your judgement, whatever is acquired before the fight and the indivisible remnants.'[2]

In return for receiving these privileges, a tribal leader would assume financial responsibility for the family of any member of his tribe who loses his life in the raid. By their nature, Arabs were generous; they used to feed the poor and the needy and defame those who refused to extend the hand of assistance and financial help to those in distress. This generosity was arguably the outcome of the arid conditions they lived in, in addition to their general good nature, fostered by simple desert life, which confined their concerns to the necessities of life and encouraged them to diminish their attachment to any luxuries.[3] Their view of money and the tribal structure of their society contributed to this since,

1 M. Lecker, 'Pre-Islamic Arabia', in *The New Cambridge History of Islam*, ed. C. F. Robinson (Cambridge: Cambridge University Press, 2010), 153; J. A. C. Brown, 'The Social Context of Pre-Islamic Poetry: Poetic Imagery and Social Reality in the *Mu'allaqat*', *Arab Studies Quarterly* 25, no. 3 (2003): 29–50.

2 A. M. al-Sallabī, *al-Sīra al-nabawiyya: Durūs wa-'ibar* (Mansoura: Maktabat al-Īmān, 2006), 33; A. B. Q. al-Aṣma'ī, *al-Aṣma'iyyāt: The Selections of al-Aṣma'ī* (Cairo: Dār al-Ma'ārif, 2011), 37.

3 A. Ibn Khaldūn, *The Muqaddimah: An Introduction to History* (Beirut: Dār al-Fikr, 2005), 67.

> [L]iving in the arid desert where drought covered most of the year, they did not have access to food, something which created an imperative to solidarity between them. With this, they viewed money as a means not an end, a means to honourable life and doing good deeds. Their generosity was a confirmation of their social belonging and a necessity of living in a tribal society where the individual ego dissolves in the communal entity.[4]

It should not be thought, however, that such a charitable and generous attitude was driven solely by sincere altruism; they used it as a source of pride and social self-image. A tribe or an individual would find fame and pride when a poet commemorated their charitable acts by mentioning them in a poem. In a society that celebrated poetry and bravery, this meant a form of advertising the act and ennobling the name of the individual or the tribe concerned. They consciously sought for their names to be immortalised through their deeds, which were to be kept in the quasi-historical record of poetry. Undertaking precisely this function, the poet al-Ḥārith ibn Ḥilliza al-Yashkurī depicts the generosity of a tribal leader:

يحبوك بالزَّعف الفيوض على * هِميانها والدُّهم كالغَرْسِ

وبالسبيك الصُّفر يُضعِفها * وبالبغايا البيض واللُّعس

لا يرتجي للمال يُهلكه * سعدُ النجوم إليه كالنحس

فله هنالك لا عليه إذا * دَنِعَت أنوف القوم للتعس

He will grace you with perfect armours, overflowing
 on their waist-belts and tall horses
With minted gold which he doubles, and with
 white and black-lipped female slaves
He is not afraid of spending money; good days
 and bad days to him are alike
So prayer will be his, not against him, when others
 will be dispraised for their failure[5]

---

4 M. A. al-Mubayyidin and I. O. Barhumah, *Aspects of the Social Life in the Book of Mufadhaliyat* (Jordan: Mutah University Deanship of Academic Research, 2007), 4.

5 A. al-Dabbī, *al-Mufaḍḍaliyyāt* (Cairo: Dār al-Maʿārif, 2010), 133–34.

On a few occasions, this generosity also extended to manumitting slaves as a gesture of goodwill.[6]

However, there are three essential observations about these charitable gestures that restricted their efficacy at levels of coverage and continuity; thus, they remained intermittent, individualistic and clannish. This paper will highlight these three obstacles and lay the groundwork as to why they developed in the pre-Islamic Arabian society and what procedures were introduced by the Prophet to handle them. The first observation is the absence of balance and planning in spending. A typical Arab would give whatever was within their means to the guests and help those in distress, even if that left him bankrupt. The untamed desire for spending or giving, even if it led to neglecting one's own family duties, would often result in social complications. Frequently, for example, a wife who would see her husband helping outside in a way that jeopardised family finances, and move from verbal blame to requesting divorce, as the husband's unchecked generosity would otherwise leave her and her children totally neglected.[7] Al-Muraqqash al-Saghīr Rabī'a ibn Sa'd b. Malik describes his own experience thus:

آذنت جارتي بوشك رحيلي * باكرا جاهرت بخطب جليل

أزمعت بالفراق لما رأتني * أَتلِفُ المالَ لا يذَمّ دخيلي

أربعي إنما يريبك مني * إرثَ مجد وجِدٌّ لبٌّ أصيل

عجباً ما عجبت للعاقد المالَ * وريبُ الزمان جمٌّ الخبول

ويُضيعُ الذي يصيرُ إليه * من شقاءٍ أو ملك خلدٍ بجيل

أجمِلْ العيشَ إنّ رزقَكَ آتٍ * لا يردُّ الترقيح شروى فتيلِ

My spouse announced her soon departure;
tomorrow, what distressing news

6 M. Ibrahim, 'Social and Economic Conditions in Pre-Islamic Arabia', *International Journal of Middle East Studies* 14 (1982): 346.

7 al-Dabbi, *al-Mufaḍḍaliyyāt*, 250.

She decided to leave me when she had seen me spend all
    my money to avoid the dispraise of my guest
Relax, I say, what distresses you is indeed my
    glorious generosity and genuine nobility
What should really cause distress is a man who withholds
    money, only for life's troubles to take it away
They will wipe away whatever he achieves, whether
    misfortune or a great kingdom
Rest assured, your sustenance will inevitably come to you;
    withholding money does not save you the tiniest trouble[8]

The second observation is limitedness in scope and intermittence. Arabian charity focussed on feeding the hungry or, more accurately, sharing food as and when the needy appeared: there was not an already established fund for people to take from all the time; rather, it was a 'give-as-you-go' activity.[9] There was not much regard for any need beyond that; at times of cold wind or calamity, they would welcome seekers of help but, oftentimes, restrict it to family networks due to the inability to cover an extended number of needy individuals. Arabs considered the act of 'offering food' (*iṭʿām al-ṭaʿām*) as the epitome of their charitable ventures.[10] Furthermore, there is no indication of any devotional significance in that, since they used to make sacrificial offerings to their idols. Al-Jāhiz highlights this as he relates that Hāshim boasted his own superiority over the rest of the Quraysh for being 'the most who fed the poor' and that the 'best form of charity is to offer food that one has'.[11] The joften discontinuous and limited coverage of such activities is noticeable from the lack of any reference in literary sources to other charitable activities beyond that, which arguably indicates why the Arabs held the act of 'feeding' in such high regard. At times of difficulty, however, they would drop these activities of extended help and limit their assistance to very close circles due to the scarcity of resources and the individualistic nature of their charitable initiatives. Brown casts doubt on any poetry that claims the continuation of their generous food-sharing at times of famine and aridness and ascribes this to their fascination with hyperbolic

8 Ibid., 251.
9 Brown, 'Social Context of Pre-Islamic Poetry', 41.
10 Ibid.
11 al-Jāhiz, *al-Bukhalāʾ* (Cairo: Dār al-Maʿārif, 2009), 230.

self-imaging that is divorced from reality at times.[12] In their study, Dirks et al. confirm this universal pattern of behaviour exhibited during times of food shortage, and how hunger intertwined with danger fashions the character of many populations and leads them to reduce their societal bonds of extended food-sharing to the very limited family circle, promoting a 'sociology of hoarding'.[13] In light of such human behaviour, we can understand that any talk about generosity at times of famine remains merely plausible and was only limited to times of ease and fertility; while difficulty led to a fall in their generosity, their poetic boasting continued, anachronistically, to be on the rise.[14]

What one observes is the lack of institutionalisation and futuristic vision for sustainability. The composition of Arabian society, of blood-bonded tribes or alliances and their non-sedentary lifestyle as nomads, semi-nomads or, to a lesser degree, settled populations, makes it all-the-more difficult to imagine how charitable activities could be organised in such collective entities.[15] Tribal federations and alliances were mainly military and involved lengthy warfare; they had little thought and time to spare for proper initiatives to regulate the individual, spontaneous charitable activities or create an institutional entity to sustain them. As Sadr rightly notes, 'ignorance was a culture that not only influenced the livelihood and the economy of the Arabs, but also had a considerable effect on their visions and thoughts'.[16] Another factor that contributed to this lack of institutionalisation was the limited number of literate people in Arabia.[17] The ability to write and document financial deals and money matters was quite uncommon, especially in central Arabia. As questionable as it may seem, it can be argued that it allowed space for people to display their personal honesty and integrity. In a society that paid a lot of attention to these qualities, word of mouth was a powerful tool of giving credit to certain people and discrediting others. Orality, rather than writing, was the principal, defining feature of human communication in general and people resorted to script as a later necessity.[18]

12 Brown, 'Social Context of Pre-Islamic Poetry', 42.

13 R. Dirks, G. J. Armelagos, C. A. Bishop et al., 'Social Responses during Severe Food Shortages and Famine', *Current Anthropology* 21 (1980): 28.

14 Brown, 'Social Context of Pre-Islamic Poetry', 42.

15 Lecker, 'Pre-Islamic Arabia', 153; S. K. Sadr, *The Economic System of the Early Islamic Period: Institutions and Policies* (New York: Palgrave MacMillan, 2016), 5.

16 Sadr, *Economic System*, 20.

17 Lecker, 'Pre-Islamic Arabia', 157.

18 Q. al-Sāmurrā'ī, *Arabic Islamic Palaeography and Codicology* (Riyadh: King Faisal Center for Research and Islamic Studies, 2001) 23; Ibn Khaldūn, *Muqaddimah*, 327.

2. A New Phase in Arabia: Establishing the City-State

The city of Yathrib, later known as Medina, hosted the first city-state in central Arabia. After a long turbulent political history,[19] the city started to enjoy harmony and feel the blessing of a civic society where people were entitled to their faiths and communal traditions, yet required to collaborate in defending the emerging city-state against foreign attacks and contribute to making it a stronger, peaceful and exemplary place. The newly founded social model maintained the familial, tribal and communal ties as positive powers within society, but also introduced new notions of central government and fought to eradicate the racial discrimination and blind loyalties (*'aṣabiyya*) that were common in pre-Islamic Arabia. In attempts of fostering the entity of the new city-state, geographical borders of Medina were drawn, a penal code was set out to maintain order and safety and fiscal duties were distributed amongst the residents of the city who had agreed to join what was then known as the Charter of Medina. Joining such a charter was voluntary; it brought about advantages in the same manner as it imposed responsibilities. This constitution claims the merit of establishing a multicultural society in the midst of those uncivilised peoples where equality, cooperation, justice, respect and the rule of law became, for the first time, central themes in human interaction.[20] Through the application of diplomacy and enterprise, Medina witnessed continuous prosperity, so much so that the per capita income of most Muslims had grown remarkably enabling many of them to pay *zakāt*.[21] More importantly, a financial system to manage public funds (with a focus on charity and similar state revenues), ensure transparency, sustainability and wise spending, and appropriate taxation though *zakāt* was developed and efficiently applied. The following is an account of the features of this system through which it not only treated the failures in the previous scattered charitable activities but also put in place unprecedented foundations for subsequent Islamic governments to build on.

19 See J. R. Cole, *Muhammad: Prophet of Peace amid the Clash of Empires* (New York: Nation Books, 2018), 94; Sadr, *Economic System*, 12.

20 H. M. al-Qādirī, *The Constitution of Madinah, the American, the British and the European Constitutions: An Analytical Comparative Study* (Kuwait: Dār al-Ḍiyā', 2018), 106.

21 B. Koehler, 'The Economist Mohammed Ibn Abdullah (570–632)', *Economic Affairs* 31, no. 1 (2011): 110; Sadr, *Economic System*, 94.

3. Prophetic Work on Money Matters for Public Benefit

I argue that the best way to approach the multifaceted Prophetic initiatives to manage public money is to investigate the procedures introduced to manage, account and track money at different stages. For an understanding of the systematic flow of public money, I propose three stages: public resources (this includes the collection of *zakāt* and other financial dues from their resources and details of ensuring the efficiency and transparency of this process); public funds (storing, accounting and tracking the collected money to mitigate embezzlement and misappropriation); and public spending (planning future spending of the funds, prioritising needs and creating sustainable projects to ensure perpetual, long-term and maximised benefit for the whole society). In each of these stages, transparency, professionalism and maximisation of benefit were the overarching themes that guided the shift towards institutionalisation. The following diagram helps in visualising these stages and their respective procedures, which are discussed in the sections below.

3.1 Resources

At this stage, the Prophetic focus was on estimating the *zakāt*-able and taxable monies (assets, crops, etc.) to facilitate the calculation of dues, then documenting the assets and the levied money for future reference or disputes and creating a hierarchical variety of roles to carry out these different jobs.

— *Estimation*

The Arabic word for estimating crops ahead of the harvest is *kharṣ*. In this process, a professional *khāriṣ* (estimator) moves from one date tree or vine tree to another estimating how many dry dates, grapes or mature grains to expect from the yet-to-mature moist dates, grapes or immature grains. Al-Kittānī relates in this regard from Ibn Abī Ḥumayd, 'On our way to Tabūk with the Messenger of God, we passed by the valley of al-Qura and came across an orchard that was owned by a woman. The Prophet said to us, "Estimate," and we estimated it and he estimated it after us as 10 *awsuq* (600 *ṣāʿ*[22]) and said to

22 A traditional measurement that is composed of 4 mudd. In modern measurement, 1 *ṣāʿ* is 2.7 litres. See A. Mubārak, *al-Mīzān fī al-aqyisa wa-l-makāyīl wa-l-awzān* (Cairo: Arabic Language Academy, 2011).

the woman, "Make sure it is ready for us when we come back to you."'[23] This report depicts the authenticity and meticulous process of the estimation process as the Prophet himself repeated it after his Companions to eliminate any possibility of error. Estimation covered a variety of crops which were *zakāt*-able, noting that cultivating perishable crops and vegetables was limited in scale and, since they are not *zakāt*-able, they were not included in the estimation.[24] It was also carried out by a list of professional estimators who were selected by the Prophet, including ʿAbd Allāh ibn Rawāḥa, ʿAttab ibn Usayd, Sahl ibn Abī Ḥathama, al-Ṣalt ibn Maʿdikarib and Farwa ibn ʿAmr ibn Wadaqa al-Biyaḍī. It was also carried out in various locations including Medina and Khaybar. To facilitate the process of estimation and subsequent documentation, calibration was standardised and clear injunctions, warning of any fraudulent interference in measures, were announced by the Prophet himself through his sayings and through the Qurʾan, in addition to appointing a state executive known as *al-muḥtasib* to inspect, among other things, weights and measures to ensure they were in accordance with state standards.[25] In this mainly agrarian economy, measuring was an essential tool to ensure fair and efficient collection and distribution. *Mudd*, *ṣāʿ*, *faraq*, *wasaq* and *ʿaraq* were amongst the standardised and calibrated measures. Eighty *wasaq* of dates and 20 *wasaq* of barley were the yearly share of the Prophet's wives collectively.[26]

— *Documentation*

Recording *zakāt*-able assets and amounts was necessary to facilitate the process of collection in subsequent years. Contemporary financial institutions use past figures to project future ones and thus build budgets and decide on public spending. With this procedure in place, there was no deficit in the annual budget throughout the time of the Prophet and early caliphs.[27] Al-Kittānī notes that

23 al-Kittānī, *al-Tarātīb al-idāriyya wa-l-ʿamālāt wa-ṣināʿāt wa-l-matājir wa-l-ḥāla al-ʿilmiyya* (Beirut: Dār al-Bashāʾir al-Islāmiyya, 2013), 487.

24 Sadr, *Economic System*, 96.

25 M. A. Khan, *Economic Teachings of Prophet Muhammad: A Select Anthology of Hadith Literature on Economics* (Islamabad: International Institute of Islamic Economic and Institute of Policy Studies, 1989), 167; A. Murtuza and W. Abdallah, 'Islamic *Muhtasib* and American CPAs: A Comparative Study of Institutions Meant to Protect Public Interest', *Journal of Accounting, Business & Management* 14 (2007): 42; Koehler, 'The Economist', 110.

26 al-Kittānī, *al-Tarātīb al-idāriyya*, 605.

27 Sadr, *Economic System*, 126.

charity, *zakāt* and public money used to be recorded by specialists appointed by the Prophet so that such a process would occur under direct guidance from the Prophet himself.[28] Jahm ibn al-Ṣalt and Ḥudhayfa ibn al-Yamān would replace al-Zubayr ibn al-ʿAwwām in recording *sadaqāt* when the latter was unavailable. In another narration, Jahm and Zubayr would record while Ḥudhayfa would be carrying out the estimation. The increase in the number of literate people in Medina – due to Prophetic educational projects – contributed immensely to the success of these activities. It is important to highlight here that while documentation was a means to record money, it had encouraged many Companions to achieve the required knowledge that enabled them to carry out this role, thereby enhancing the community's overall level of literacy and promoted knowledge of calculation in addition to utilising qualified individuals and creating employment opportunities.[29] The scope of recording also included debts, transactions and pledges, whether personal or communal. Al-ʿAlā' ibn ʿUqba, al-Arqam ibn Abī al-Arqam, al-Ḥuṣayn ibn Numayr and al-Mughīra ibn Shuʿba were employed for this department.[30]

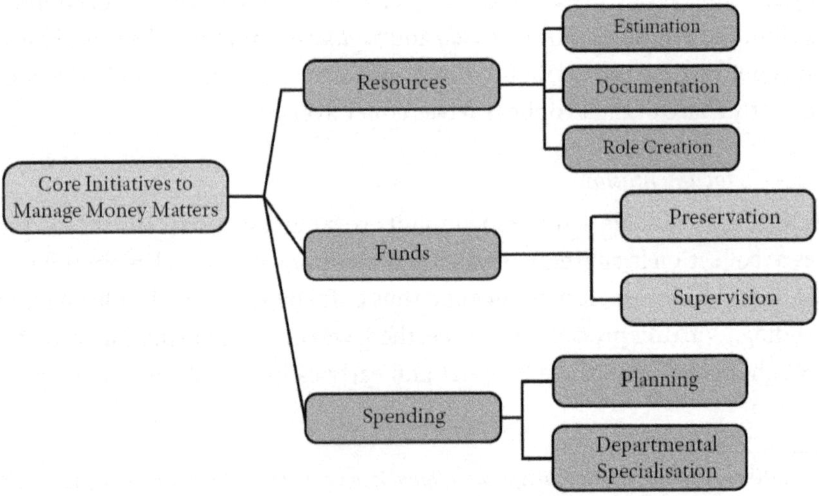

— *Role Creation*

The multi-departmental fiscal institution required an army of civil servants

28 al-Kittānī, *al-Tarātīb al-idāriyya*, 586.

29 A. S. U. al-Muḥammadī, *Akhlāqiyyāt al-taʾāmul al-iqtiṣādī fī al-fikr al-Islāmī* (Amman: Dār al-Nūr, 2014), 108.

30 al-Kittānī, *al-Tarātīb al-idāriyya*, 440.

working in different specialisations, from collection and sorting to documenting and distributing. Al-Kittānī mentions some of these distinctive functions created by the Prophet and the names of individuals who occupied each one of them. I will mention four of them here: (a) *jizya* (poll tax) administrator: '*Jizya* was collected from non-Muslims who lived under the protection of a Muslim government but did not wish to become Muslims and was levied in return of economic, social and welfare services offered to them in addition for protecting their lives and property and, in a great sense, it was similar to Zakat Al-Fitr which was paid by Muslims annually.'[31] Mu'ādh ibn Jabal and Abū 'Ubayda ibn al-Jarrāḥ were amongst the people who were nominated for this role; (b) tither: tithe is a business or trade tax levied upon non-Muslims in recompense of trading in Muslims lands. Many Companions were given this responsibility, including a woman who asked the Prophet whether she should start collecting tithes from her tribe or not;[32] (c) land-tax administrator: this new role was also occupied by many people, including Sawād ibn Ghaziyya al-Anṣārī; (d) *zakāt* collectors, also known as *al-muṣaddiqīn* (sing. *al-muṣaddiq*): this role is arguably wider in scope and responsibility, and, therefore, necessitated the creation of a hierarchy of *zakāt* collectors, local and regional, all reporting to the central authority. Quoting al-Kalā'ī, al-Kittānī names amongst them Ḥudhayfa ibn al-Yamān, Khālid ibn Sa'īd ibn al-'Āṣ, 'Adī ibn Ḥātim al-Ṭā'ī, al-Zabraqan ibn Badr al-Tamīmī, Mu'ādh ibn Jabal, 'Umar ibn al-Khaṭṭāb, Sahl ibn Minjāb and Rāfi' ibn Mukayth al-Juhanī. Notably, clear instructions were given to every *muṣaddiq* to administer complete fairness and strict adherence to the code of conduct particular to that job. Khuzayma ibn 'Āṣim was given a letter of appointment along with instructions to treat the community to whom he was sent fairly and professionally. Compliance with the given instructions and setting the standard for professionalism was common amongst the *muṣaddiqīn*. Al-Kittānī relates a story of one of the *muṣaddiqīn* refusing to take a highly valued she-camel offered by a *zakāt* payer out of compliance with Prophetic instructions to accept only an average-value camel because accepting or selecting expensive ones forfeits the purpose of *zakāt*, which instead aims at encouraging the rich to give to society rather than punishing them by stripping them of the best parts of their wealth.[33]

31 Sadr, *Economic System*, 105.

32 J. A. D. Ibn Manẓūr, *Lisān al-'Arab* (Beirut: Dār Ṣādir, 2006), 10:157.

33 al-Kittānī, *al-Tarātīb al-idāriyya*, 586.

3.2 Funds

Two steps were employed to deal with the collected funds: preservation, via recording or filing them as public money, and supervising and monitoring this process through bookkeeping and accountability. This also required a hierarchy of administration to ensure transparency and prevent misappropriation. Below, I will give details of the necessary steps to achieve these two goals: namely, preservation and supervision.

— *Preservation*

The Prophet appointed trustees to preserve the wealth of orphans and others to guard public funds after they had been collected. ʿAbd Allāh ibn Kaʿb al-Anṣārī was appointed to preserve the fifth (*khums*) while Abū Ḥurayra was entrusted with *zakāt al-fiṭr*. Amongst the individuals appointed as trustees over the wealth of orphans was ʿUthmān ibn ʿAffān, ʿAbd al-Raḥmān ibn ʿAwf and al-Miqdād ibn al-Aswad. They handled this wealth effectively and were ready with accounts, as and when requested. One remarkable procedure taken to ensure preservation of public money was branding (*wasm*) or marking charity camels. There was a specific stamp or marker for charity camels so that no one milked or took them thinking they were privately owned. This would also help in returning these camels should any of them stray into the desert. This procedure is similar to stamping books in libraries and other public properties today to prevent people from stealing and keeping them as their own.

— *Supervision*

The Prophet employed strict accountability and auditing procedures to prevent mishandling of money and fund embezzlement. One important job that was introduced is the role of *al-mustawfī*, who was sent by the central government to collect *zakāt* funds from local *zakāt* collectors and ensure that the accounts were accurate. This job, which combined accounting and administrative powers, was occupied by ʿAlī ibn Abī Ṭālib at one time and by Ḥājib ibn Zurāra al-Tamīmī at another. Another equally important post is *al-muḥāsib*, which is more of an auditing nature. The Prophet carried out auditing at least once himself when a *zakāt* administrator from the tribe of al-Azd presented the *zakāt* funds of Banū Salīm and claimed that a certain portion of the funds was given to him as a gift. The Prophet refused the man's claim and dismissed the permissibility that such side-lined funds can be treated as personal gifts. A civil servant, the Prophet established, cannot accept gifts from the public as this is bribery in disguise.

This strict policy of dealing with public money extended to the Prophet's own family, who were no exception to the rules of preservation and protection. Sadr, calling it 'wizards of kinsfolk', reiterates the importance of eradicating any means of a governor's relatives invading public money to dry out corruption and terminate any possible plundering.[34] Koehler supports this through a practical example of handling endowment as the Prophet 'once spotted his grandson Hassan eating a fruit from a tree that had been given to provide food for the poor. He scooped the fruit from the boy's mouth and scolded him…'[35]

3.3 Spending

This refers to the management of public funds to ensure they are spent for the right purposes, used in services that are delivered to all sectors of society, sustained in such a way that they are not depleted and protected from unwise or unmonitored spending. In this area, the Prophetic initiatives and measures peaked. Procedures taken here not only reflect the Prophet's administrative foresight but also prove his creative fiscal model of maximising benefit and widening reach. The discussion below will focus on two procedures that helped achieve the above goals; namely, planning and departmental differentiation.

— *Planning*

The Prophet introduced a procedure unknown in Arabia before him: the public registry or census. Various types of public registries were introduced, including a members of the army registry and a general population registry.[36] Narrations confirm that he requested his registrars to write down the names of every member of the Muslim community. At another instance, he requested the names of everyone who joined the army. He used this information to build a welfare system in which everyone's basic needs were covered from public money.[37] Members of the army were paid and their families were taken care of while the general population received help in accordance to their needs and responsibilities. A married man would be given twice as much as a single

34 See Sadr, *Economic System*, 86.

35 B. Koehler, 'Muhammad's Conception of Property as a Bundle of Rights', *Economic Affairs* 35 (2015): 54.

36 See Sadr, *Economic System*, 71–72; A. H. al-Balādhūrī, *Futūḥ al-buldān* (Beirut: Dār al-Kutub al-ʿIlmiyya, 1983), 42.

37 Sadr, *Economic System*, 119.

man, and children were also allocated a form of maintenance benefit. I have mentioned before that land registry was also useful, serving as a track record of asset movement to ensure fiscal dues were levied accurately and on time. The keyword here is *planning* the resources and the beneficiaries. Al-Kittānī confirms the existence of written warrants in the hands of people stating how much each one should receive from the public money.[38] Following the Prophet's demise, Abū Bakr requested that these parchments be re-endorsed under his reign; a government document renewal of sorts. Lists of givers and recipients were always available at the Prophet's time. Needless to stress here that the legal categorisation of *zakāt* beneficiaries presents in itself a road map to any subsequent funds distribution as it sets out priorities and areas of focus. Whether able to earn or not, an individual who qualifies legally as poor was entitled access to *zakāt*.[39] To ensure efficacy, any modern procedure of dealing public funds draws a map of sectors or spots that need work and creates a list of priorities before moving to the actual distribution of funds.

Another area that displays excellent management is how endowments (*awqāf*; sing. *waqf*) were managed. Endowments were registered and owned by the *waqf* entity but the income from these endowments were due to beneficiaries. The Prophet granted to his Companions 'legal title over the lands yet imposed constraints on how they could use income derived from it and making the distribution of benefit subject to legal oversight'.[40] So while the Companions had the land, they had to abide by a condition – that proceeds go to public welfare. Koehler notes that this secured independence as it ring-fenced capital assets 'from the control by a secular or religious authority'. In this way, two birds were killed with one stone: he complied with the Qur'anic injunctions of giving charity and secured the independent administration of endowment. When endowments fall within the administrative circles of government or religious authorities, 'no institutional checks and balances [are] there to afford protection against authorities absorbing and consolidating endowments'.[41] In short, he empowered civic philanthropy in a legally autonomous model, at once creative and unprecedented. In recent times, endowments in Muslim

38 al-Kittānī, *al-Tarātīb al-idāriyya*, 382.

39 M. B. A. Mayyara, *al-Durr al-thamīn wa-l-mawrid al-mu'īn* (Tunisia: al-Jam'iyya al-Tūnisiyya li-Iḥyā' al-Turāth al-Zaytūnī, 2011), 2:713; M. B. A. Ibn Juzayy, *al-Qawānīn al-fiqhiyya* (Beirut: Dār Ibn Ḥazm, 2013), 200.

40 Koehler, 'Muhammad's Conception of Property', 55.

41 Ibid.

countries were swallowed up by the state under the guise of nationalisation and, therefore, their role died out and their power shrank.

— *Departmental Specialisation*

One may also use 'differentiation' in place of 'specialisation', as what is meant here is that the Prophet created a system where no one individual or group is continually and single-handedly responsible for the spending of public funds. Practically, this led to assigning specific spending and budgeting responsibilities to a variety of departments, individuals or experts and, therefore, ensuring wise spending and eliminating or reducing mismanagement. Just like funds, proper allocation of duties secures sustainability.[42] Al-Kittānī lists three categories of spending agents/departments: one is the private spender, another is the public budgeter and purchases department and the third is the special mission agent. A private spender, also known as *amīn ṣā'ir*, was responsible for the expenses of the Prophet and his family. Just like any modern state, a president has allowances and specific expenses and, due to the sensitive nature of his role, he is supposed to delegate his finances to an advisor or top administrator. This function was occupied by Bilāl.[43] A public spender is a type of treasurer who oversees general expenses, while a private or special mission is someone who is entrusted with a mission or a project within certain parameters. While Marwān ibn al-Jidhʿ was, at one instance, a public spender, ʿAlī ibn Abī Ṭālib was assigned to carry wergild and other funds and travel to Banū Judhayma to reconcile their feuding parties. A similar mission included ʿAbd Allāh ibn ʿAmr al-Khuzāʿī, who carried financial help to the Meccans by the command of the Prophet before the conquest of Mecca; notably, he was asked to find someone to accompany him in this dangerous mission as well. This differentiation brought forth further growth and expansion of these departments, from being composed of one person to becoming more efficient bodies.

Conclusion

Prophetic initiatives to institutionalise public money in his city-state of Medina were creative and unprecedented. Alongside other administrative arrangements of the emerging society, they displayed wide knowledge of not only how to run a

42 See M. N. Aziz and O. Bin Mohamad, 'Islamic Social Business to Alleviate Poverty and Social Inequality', *International Journal of Social Economics* 43 (2016): 582.

43 See Sadr, *Economic System*, 120; al-Kittānī, *al-Tarātīb al-idāriyya*, 640.

state, but how to set up a model of efficacy and professionalism. The undertaken procedures also practically cemented the Islamic ethos of transparency, honesty and accountability and moved them from mere theoretical discourse to a living reality. It is essential to note that diverse economists, ranging from Max Weber to Robert Barro, pointed out the link between religion or faith and economic organisation;[44] the latter can, in many ways, help in discerning the efficiency of the ethical system of the former. *Zakāt* and other funds were precisely accrued, monitored and spent. This unprecedented mechanism shifted the concept of charity from an activity to satiate the hunger of the poor or alleviate their pain to becoming a visionary procedure that empowers the poor to become rich and self-sufficient through creating opportunities and sustainable projects.[45] From Prophetic practice, Muslim jurists concluded that providing capital or buying tools for a poor person to start earning, if they have the ability, was a valid cause to spend the collected funds upon.[46]

Although a great deal of literature is available on juristic solutions for the problem of poverty and how the institutions of *zakāt* and public funds evolved throughout Muslim history, this topic, of the systemisation of money matters during the Prophet's lifetime, has not been duly treated. Apart from the work of Sayyid ʿAbd al-Ḥayy al-Kittānī, I have not come across a dedicated, comprehensive and detailed study on the topic. Further studies, moreover, will help Western Muslims explore avenues to maximise their utilisation of *zakāt* and charity funds in their social context. It will also show that accounting, auditing and accountability standards were ingrained in the Muslim community from its earliest days and are not foreign to Islam;[47] this will open avenues for wider social discussion in the diverse context Muslims live in. At a time when aspersions are directed to the financial integrity and efficiency of some Muslim charities, there is no better cure than highlighting and enforcing these Prophetic measures of transparency and balance; this, I would argue, is a real reform from within the tradition that renders borrowed solutions redundant. In terms of faith, further studies will shed much needed light on this rarely visited area of the life of the Prophet and undo the continuous misrepresentation of his person in the media.

44 See Koehler, 'The Economist', 109.

45 See K. Hadwī, *Zakāt al-amwāl al-mujammada fī al-fiqh al-Mālikī* (Morocco: Ministry of Endowments and Islamic Affairs, 2017), 355; Sadr, *Economic System*, 108.

46 See Hadwī, *Zakāt al-amwāl*, 358.

47 See Murtuza and Abdallah, 'Islamic Muhtasib', 42.

ALI FANAEI

Religious Tax as a Source of Income for Religious Study: A New Approach towards the Problem and Its Solution[1]

Objectivity and honesty constitute the core of academic integrity and are central virtues in any kind of study, including religious study in seminaries. Like other scholars, religious scholars should be objective and honest if their research is to be epistemically valid and reliable, and their findings authoritative and binding for their followers. In other words, the epistemic authority of religious scholars is dependent upon their objectivity in discovering religious truths and their honesty in disclosing the results of their research to laypeople.

To be objective means to be free from bias by having an impartial attitude towards all possible conclusions and not to have any personal or group interest favouring a specific outcome without sufficient evidence. Objectivity requires that one's research is conducted with an epistemically suitable motive, such as finding the truth as it is. The adage 'We are the sons of evidence, and hence we are inclined to whatever our mother is inclined to' refers to this sense of objectivity, and the right reason for conducting research.

Honesty in this context means revealing to others the outcome of the research as it is, when there is no more important moral duty, such as saving the life of an innocent or reducing the sever suffering of others. A morally virtuous scholar is someone who does not hide or manipulate the findings of his research to protect his own personal or group interest. Although honesty in this sense is a 'qualified' moral duty, the qualification by which a moral duty is qualified is itself another moral duty, which is of more importance from a moral point of view. Therefore, we should acknowledge that there is a morally significant difference between hiding the truth from others for the sake of a more important moral reason, such as saving the life of innocents, and hiding it from them for the sake of an immoral reason, such as personal interest or an even less important moral reason.

---

1 I would like to express my gratitude to the participants of the 7th Contemporary Fiqhī Issues Workshop (Al-Mahdi Institute, 4–5 July 2019) for their useful questions and comments, and to my colleague Dr Wahid M. Amin for reviewing my article and suggesting improvements.

However, there are some obstacles in conducting research responsibly, and these obstacles are not peculiar to research about non-religious issues. Perhaps one of the most pervasive and widespread of these obstacles is what is called 'the conflict of interest'. The literature on the conflict of interest as an ethical and legal issue is quite extensive, especially in domains such as medical research.[2] I employ the term in a technical sense, by which I mean a situation where the personal or group interests of a scholar conflict with his academic virtues and obligations. One obvious instance of such a situation is the case in which finding the truth and/or disclosing it to others is in conflict with the financial interest of the researcher or his academic institution. Conflict of interest prevents scholars from maintaining their integrity, following academic virtues and discharging their academic duties. It is very difficult, if not impossible, for a scholar to remain objective and honest when his own personal or group interest is at stake, and it is quite reasonable to not trust the judgement or testimony of someone who is in such a situation.

2 See, for example, P. L. Romain, 'Conflicts of Interest in Research: Looking Out for Number One Means Keeping the Primary Interest Front and Center', *Current Reviews in Musculoskeletal Medicine* 8, no. 2 (2015): 122–27; D. F. Thompson, 'Understanding Financial Conflicts of Interest', *New England Journal of Medicine* 329 (1993): 573–76; C. R. MacKenzie and B. N. Cronstein, 'Conflict of Interest', *HSS Journal* 2, no. 2 (2006): 198–201; D. B. Resnik, 'Institutional Conflicts of Interest in Academic Research', *Science and Engineering Ethics* 25, no. 6 (2019): 1661–69; M. J. Field and B. Lo, eds, *Conflict of Interest in Medical Research, Education, and Practice* (Washington, DC: National Academies Press, 2009); J. E. Bekelman, Y. Li and C. P. Gross, 'Scope and Impact of Financial Conflicts of Interest in Biomedical Research: A Systematic Review', *Jama* 289, no. 4 (2003): 454–65; B. A. Goldrick, E. Larson and D. Lyons, 'Conflict of Interest in Academia', *Image: The Journal of Nursing Scholarship* 27, no. 1 (1995): 65–69; S. Lipton, E. Boyd and L. Bero, 'Conflicts of Interest in Academic Research: Policies, Processes, and Attitudes', *Accountability in Research: Policies and Quality Assurance* 11, no. 2 (2004): 83–102; P. J. Friedman, 'The Troublesome Semantics of Conflict of Interest', *Ethics & Behavior* 2, no. 4 (1992): 245–51; P. J. Friedman, 'The Impact of Conflict of Interest on Trust in Science', *Science and Engineering Ethics* 8, no. 3 (2002): 413–20; H. Brody, 'Clarifying Conflict of Interest', *The American Journal of Bioethics* 11, no. 1 (2011): 23–28; and R. S. Saver, 'Is It Really All about the Money? Reconsidering Non-financial Interests in Medical Research', *The Journal of Law, Medicine & Ethics* 40, no. 3 (2012): 467–81.

1. Conflict of Interest in Religious Studies

Regarding religious studies, we are faced with a more specific instance of the conflict of interest when religious taxes, such as the share of the infallible Imam in *khums*, is being relied upon as the source of income by scholars. The central question of this article is whether relying upon such a source of income undermines the objectivity and honesty of religious scholars. That is, is it possible for religious scholars to sustain their academic integrity and remain objective and honest whilst relying on religious tax as the source of their income? In what follows, I will explore, compare and critically examine two answers to this question put forward by two contemporary religious reformists in Iran, namely, the late Ayatollah Morteza Motahhari and Dr Abdulkarim Soroush.

Motahhari and Soroush provide different answers to our central question.[3] According to Motahhari, the answer is no, provided that the religious tax is collected and distributed *indirectly*. According to Soroush, the answer is yes. They both agree that something is wrong with the current situation of religious studies in Shi'ite seminaries. They disagree, however, about the exact cause of the problem and its proper solution. Both agree that the source of income would have a huge influence upon the moral integrity of religious scholars and may undermine their objectivity and honesty. This common assumption is based on their realistic anthropology, according to which religious scholars are no different from other scholars and average laypeople in that they are not infallible, and therefore may harbour ulterior motives that lead to misconduct in research. If in some cases personal virtues such as piety prevent religious scholars from misconduct in their research, it is quite accidental and extraordinary. Therefore, they both agree that we need a more effective and systematic solution. In the following, I will elaborate on their solutions respectively and will try to show that their solutions are not effective and why.

3 M. Motahhari, 'The Fundamental Problem in the Clerical Establishment', in *The Most Learned of the Shi'a: The Institution of the Marja' Taqlid*, ed. Linda S. Walbridge (New York: Oxford University Press, 2001 [1962]), 161–82; A. Soroush, 'Ḥorriāt va Roḥaniyyāt', *Kian* 24 (1995): 2–11; A. Soroush, 'Sāqfe Māeishāt bar Sotoune Shāriāt', *Kian* 26 (1995): 25–31.

2. Motahhari on Populism in Religious Studies

Motahhari developed his diagnosis and solution in an article called 'The Fundamental Problem in the Clerical Establishment', originally published in 1962.[4] Although clerical establishments in Iran have undergone major reforms since then, if we accept his analysis, we must conclude that the problem still exists, and is possibly worse than it was at that time. His main concern in that article is to provide a sympathetic criticism of clerical establishments and suggest his plan for reform.

Motahhari begins his discussion by noting some advantages of traditional seminaries over modern academic institutions, and continues:

> One night in Qom about 13 years ago [1949], I had the good fortune to attend a friendly gathering of the religious authorities and scholars. Our discussion gradually turned toward the issue of the problems and deficiencies of the clerical establishment. We discussed why it was that, in the past, our centers of spiritual and religious learning offered diverse scholarly topics from Qur'anic commentary to historiography, hadith, fiqh, usul, philosophy, theology, literature, and even medicine and mathematics, whereas now the subject matter has become very limited. In other words, in the past such centers were comprehensive, having the form and function of universities. Today, they have declined into schools of jurisprudence and other fields of study that have lost their importance. [...] Indeed, I ask you why there is such silence, serenity, and macabre morbidity among us, instead of freedom, mobility, and vitality? And why is it that whoever wants to preserve his position and status is forced to keep silent and be inactive? Why is it that our educational programs are not designed to fit contemporary needs? Why do we not have enough books, essays, journals, and periodicals? [...] Why is it that as soon as our righteous and enlightened leaders have ascended to positions of authority, they lose their ability to reform, seeming to forget their previous convictions? These are only some of our many problems and deficiencies.[5]

4 The English translation of this article is partially incorrect. So, occasionally I refer to its original version, the latest edition of which was published in 2003, with my own English translation.

5 Motahhari, 'The Fundamental Problem', 164–65.

He summarises his analysis of the source of these problems as follows:

> After a while we [i.e. attendants gathered in that meeting in Qom] decided that each person would express his opinion as to what he thought was the main reason for these problems. Everyone expressed an opinion, and I, too, expressed mine. But one of the colleagues expressed an opinion that I found superior to all others, including my own. I still hold that opinion. He said that the administration of the financial affairs of the clerical establishment, along with the way in which the clergy obtain their daily livelihood, were the fundamental reasons for the defects and problems of the religious establishment. The phrase that he used was this: 'The main cause of all our problems is *sahm-i-imām* [lit. "the share of the Imam"].'[6]

Motahhari goes on to give a more comprehensive list of the problems and deficiencies in seminaries and then summarises this part of his discussion: 'Yet the gravest deficiencies in our clerical organization are the clerical budget, salaries, financial organization, and the means of obtaining a livelihood.'[7] He insists that the mere existence of such a religious tax in the Islamic legal system is not problematic. Rather, it is 'one of the wisest instructions that one can imagine'.[8] His point is that 'over time, traditions and practices concerning the implementation and uses of *sahm-i-imām* have become prevalent and have shaped our clerical institution in a particular fashion. The resulting institutional configuration has become the source of many problems and defects'.[9]

A more systematic presentation of his diagnosis would be to say that, in his opinion, the current *method* of collecting and distributing the share of the Imam has led to populism within Shi'ite seminaries, which in turn generated the other problems that he lists. 'All the corruption,' says Motahhari, 'results from clerics obtaining their livelihood *directly* from the populace, and they need to ingratiate themselves with lay contributors and to draw attention to themselves in order to meet their financial needs.'[10] 'Corruption occurs,' he adds, 'because the clerics of various cities have no choice but to turn their clerical profession

6 Ibid., 165.
7 Ibid., 169.
8 Ibid., 165.
9 Ibid.
10 Ibid., 176 (emphasis added).

into trade and use the mosques as their business offices.'[11] Thus, the natural prescription for solving the problem is to change the method of religious tax collection and distribution. All we need to do, according to Motahhari, is to collect and distribute the share of the Imam *indirectly*. He wrote: 'If this situation is correct, no one will be in *direct* contact with the populace. The eminent *marājiʿ al-taqlīd* will be freed and the mosques will not serve as business offices and trade centres anymore.'[12] And again, 'To correct these defects and problems, we must create a collective [bank] account and keep an exact tally of all transactions in the clerical centers so that no cleric can obtain his livelihood *directly* from the populace.'[13] Finally, he says: 'In our opinion, the weakening of Iran's clerical establishment is not caused by the reliance of its budget on the people's religious beliefs, but rather, it is the disorganization of this budget that has created this huge deficiency, and we can rectify this great deficiency by putting this budget in order so that the Shiʿite clerical establishment will have both power and liberty.'[14]

Comparing the clerical establishment of Iran with that of Egypt, and the religious leadership of al-Azhar, Motahhari maintains that the advantage of the latter lies in the fact that it is financially independent from religious laypeople, and, therefore, is not vulnerable to populism and enjoys freedom of thought.[15] It is easy for al-Azhar scholars to go against popular orthodoxy and issue novel and revolutionary fatwas, as is the case with Sheikh Shaltut and his famous verdict by which he acknowledged the legitimacy of following the Shiʿite legal school of thought.[16] Motahhari does not think that 'a Shiʿa clerical leader is able to issue a fatwa like [this] regardless of how openminded, reform-minded, and pious he may be'.[17] He continues: 'Even a less significant decree cannot be issued by a Shiʿa clerical leader.'[18]

The disadvantage of al-Azhar seminarians, according to Motahhari, is that, due to their financial dependency on the government, '[t]he clerical leader of Egypt will never have enough power to match that of the government, as

11 Ibid.

12 M. Motahhari, 'Moshkele Asāsi dar Sāzemāne Roḥāniyyat', in *Dah Ghooftār*, 19th ed. (Tehran: Sadrā Publishing Company, 2003), 309 (emphasis added).

13 Motahhari, 'The Fundamental Problem', 176 (emphasis added).

14 Motahhari, 'Moshkele Asāsi', 302.

15 Motahhari, 'The Fundamental Problem', 172.

16 Ibid.

17 Ibid.

18 Ibid.

occurred in the case of the tobacco issue'.[19] Motahhari states: '[w]hen a cleric relies on the populace, he gains power but loses his freedom. If he relies on the government, he loses power but maintains his freedom.'[20]

To summarise his position, Motahhari believes that the major deficiency in Shi'ite religious studies seminaries is populism, which prevents reformist leaders from making any progress. But this populism is not occasioned by using the share of the Imam as the source of income as such. Rather, it is caused by the current method of collecting and distributing that share. Based on this diagnosis, he advocates the *indirect* collection and distribution of religious tax as the solution.

However, one concern with this solution is that it shifts the problem of the conflict of interest from individual religious scholars to the organization responsible for collecting and distributing religious tax. When it comes to conflict of interest, legal persons are the same as natural persons in that they are both subject to the conflict. Nevertheless, his proposal can be seen as part of the solution if we understand it as prescribing the establishment of a regulatory body – an issue I will return to later.

3. Soroush on the Freedom of Expression in Religious Studies

As we saw earlier, Soroush agrees with Motahhari that the source of livelihood would have an enormous impact upon the objectivity and honesty of religious scholars, and, therefore, it should be avoided. His solution, however, is more radical, for his diagnosis of the source of the problem is deeper than that of Motahhari. According to Soroush, the problem at hand has nothing to do with the share of the Imam in particular. Rather, it has to do with relying on religion as a source of any worldly advantage, including financial gains. In his well-known and controversial article 'Ḥorriāt va Roḥaniyyāt' [Liberty and

19 Ibid.

20 Ibid., 172–73. He continues: 'This is true because the majority of people are faithful believers; but they are also ignorant, decadent, and uninformed. As a result, they oppose reforms. In contrast, governments, while usually openminded, are also oppressive and encroaching. The clerical establishment that depends on the populate is able to fight the oppressions and encroachments of the government, but it is unable to fight the ignorant beliefs and opinions of the people. When it depends on the government, the clerical establishment is powerful when trying to counteract the ignorant customs and thoughts of the public. It is powerless, though, when fighting against the encroachments and oppressions of the government.' Ibid., 173.

priesthood], originally published in 1995, he agrees with Motahhari that the source of income in seminaries is the root cause of all problems, but rejects the latter's proposal as insufficient, suggesting his own radical solution.

He begins by defining the 'clergy' in terms of 'those who rely on religion as the source of income'.[21] A cleric, in his definition, is someone who earns money from religion and religious activities and this common feature unifies all clergy around one axis rendering them into a social class with a particular collective identity and common professional interests.[22] Like other social groups, 'this group talks about a collective-*self* and defends this *self* against the external threats'.[23] A religious scholar, on the other hand, is someone who has an independent source of income, so that if he were to leave his religious activities, there would be no detriment to his livelihood. Unlike the clergy, religious scholars do not constitute a social class with a collective identity and common interest, and, therefore, have no fear of financial loss when expressing their academic and professional opinions.[24]

Soroush believes that Motahhari's solution is not effective 'because whenever defending the truth is tied to meeting the [legitimate or illegitimate] interests and demands of a group of people, that truth will definitely be damaged'.[25] In such a situation, 'it would become extremely difficult to separate between defending the truth and defending personal and professional interests'.[26] Therefore, Soroush concludes, '[i]t doesn't matter whether clerics earn their salary from people, or government, or a central [bank] account, because the problem is still there. In all of these cases one is making money through religion'.[27]

Based on his diagnosis, Soroush's solution is to completely separate religious affairs from financial affairs. So, religious scholars should divide their time in two: in one part, they must engage in some type of economic activity to earn their livelihood; in the second, they can devote themselves to religious study. In this way, the outcome of their research would become free from bias, because they do not need to hide or disguise religious truths in order to protect their source of income. Free and reliable religious enquiry is one in which the enquirer is not motivated by personal or professional interest.

21 Soroush, 'Ḥorriāt va Roḥaniyyāt', 2.
22 Ibid., 2–3.
23 Ibid., 3.
24 Ibid.
25 Ibid., 4.
26 Ibid.
27 Ibid.

Soroush anticipates some objections to his analysis and solution and tries to reply to them. The first objection is that 'a just and pious person is able to protect himself from falling into such a fatal trap'.[28] He replies that '[t]his is a sweet but an unfulfillable wish, because only exceptional people can practise such self-restraint, and the world is occupied and governed by average people. The history of religion supports this point'.[29] The second objection is that '[t]his is a popular way of earning money, and all experts make money from their expertise'.[30] A good example is medicine and medical experts. Physicians earn money from their profession, and this does not impair their practice or impede the progress of medical science.

Whilst accepting this last point, Soroush highlights that there is an important difference between religious and non-religious scholarly activities. The latter, says Soroush, is subject to two types of oversight that together prevent misconduct: expert and lay. However, religious scholarly activity is only subject to the expert oversight; lay oversight is impossible here, because it is based on observing the tangible consequences of the scholar's opinion, and the consequences of religious beliefs and practices only become tangible in the afterlife. According to Soroush, expert oversight is not enough by itself, since members of the relevant community of experts have a common interest that may motivate them to overlook each other's misconduct.[31]

Be this as it may, Soroush concludes that since lay oversight is impossible in religious studies we need to find another solution, and the only alternative is to completely isolate religious study as the mission of religious scholars from their source of income, so that they are not forced to follow popular opinion out of fear of losing their livelihood and their status and displeasing the clerical community.[32] In other words, religious study should be conducted for the sake of God, not for the sake of money. One cannot harbour both intentions at the same time.

I disagree with Soroush's analysis here for several reasons. First, when it comes to the conflict of interest, there is no difference between religious and non-religious scholars. The problem is the same and hence the solution, if any, would be the same.

---

28 Ibid.

29 Ibid.

30 Ibid.

31 Ibid., 4–5.

32 Ibid., 5.

Second, lay oversight is in fact not possible in many areas of scholarly research. The average person has little understanding of quantum physics, pure mathematics, nuclear medicine, economics, engineering, and so on, since the topics are so specialised, and the language incredibly technical. In fact, one could argue that for the layperson, the language of religious research is often much more accessible. And indeed, laypeople constitute the final court of judgement when it comes to understanding textual evidence, or the subject matter is something in which ordinary people are, in fact, the experts.

Third, one could argue that lay oversight is not necessarily a good criterion to judge scholarly research by, and, in fact, could have detrimental effects as the average person lacks the necessary knowledge to properly understand such research. The populism that Motahhari warned against is precisely the result of lay oversight.

Fourth, some religious practices have tangible consequences in the here and now. For example, we can measure whether religious punishments are effective in reducing crime levels, or whether the project of the Islamisation of banking has succeeded in eradicating usury, reducing the interest rate to 0 per cent, and reducing the gap between rich and poor, and so forth.

Fifth, as we saw, Soroush tries to draw a sharp distinction between the clergy and religious scholars by appealing to their definitions. But definition does not change the relevant facts. In reality, each of these two groups has its own collective identity and common interests, and both are vulnerable to conflict of interest, albeit in different ways.

And finally, Soroush's solution has been anticipated and rejected by Motahhari as an unrealistic way out. According to Motahhari,

> [W]e must consider the expansion of knowledge and the changes that have come about in the lives of people since the beginning of Islam. It has become essential that a group of people devote their entire lives to the education and administration of people's religious affairs. As a result, there is a need for a special budget to be spent wisely toward this purpose.[33]

CONCLUSION

To summarise, both Motahhari and Soroush agree that the current situation

33 Motahhari, 'The Fundamental Problem', 169.

in Shiʿite seminaries in which religious scholars depend on religious tax for their livelihood is not acceptable. Also, they concur that an internal safeguard, namely, reliance on personal virtues such as piety and abstinence, is not enough to prevent the negative impact of relying on religious tax upon the quality of religious research. They disagree, however, over the external solution.

According to Motahhari, we have no choice but to use religious tax for this purpose, though we can avoid the problem by establishing an organisation as an intermediary between the payer and the recipient of religious tax. In this way, we can prevent the opinions or inclinations of taxpayers having any influence upon the research conduct of the tax receivers.

Soroush, however, believes that Motahhari is wrong in identifying the real source of the problem, which, according to him, is relying on religious research as a source of income per se, not just direct reliance on religious tax. Therefore, the only proper and effective solution is to cut off any relationship between source of income and religious enquiry.

In my opinion, Motahhari and Soroush faltered in the first step of their endeavour, in which they were supposed to identify the nature of the problem, and the discipline to which it belongs. It seems obvious that they talk as if the problem at hand is peculiar to religious research. However, when we examine literature on 'the conflict of interest', we can clearly see that we have the exact same problem in every discipline. So, as stated before, if the problem is the same, the solution for it, if any, would be the same. The question is how to minimise or eliminate such conflict in any discipline, not just the financial conflict of interest in religious studies.

The problem under discussion is a genuine *moral* problem that has *epistemic* consequences and should be dealt with in 'research ethics'.[34] Conflict of interest arises when a person or a group has multiple interests that are mutually exclusive, so that serving and protecting some of those interests requires sacrificing the other(s). One of these mutually exclusive interests is that the person or

34 For an excellent exposition of the problem and its possible solution(s) in business, law, medicine and public policy, see D. A. Moore, D. M. Cain, G. Loewenstein and M. H. Bazerman, eds, *Conflicts of Interest: Challenges and Solutions in Business, Law, Medicine, and Public Policy* (Cambridge: Cambridge University Press, 2005). See also M. Davis and A. Stark, eds, *Conflict of Interest in the Professions* (Oxford: Oxford University Press, 2001), for the conflicts of interest in law and governance, journalism, accounting, engineering, corporate boards, academic disciplines – such as anthropology, financial services, film studies – the film industry, medical practice, correctional health services and physical therapy, and for a comparison of the conflicts of interest across professions.

group involved has an overriding professional obligation to serve and protect. The other could be financial or otherwise. The moral obligation to serve as a professional agent aims at fulfilling the ultimate end of that profession and may vary from occupation to occupation.

In academic institutions, including seminaries, the ultimate end is the integrity of research, which requires objectivity and honesty. This end will generate two moral obligations: the first is the obligation to be objective, and the second is the obligation to be honest. These moral obligations arise from the commitment that is made by taking up this occupation, but it may be followed by parallel legal and religious obligations as well as academic regulations. Therefore, misconducts of scholars are immoral behaviours that are committed when the integrity of research that they are supposed to serve and protect is unduly influenced by another interest, namely, anything that is incompatible with that interest.

The criticism that can be levelled at both Motahhari and Soroush is that the source of income is just one of multiple factors that can create a conflict of interest for all scholars including religious scholars. Other factors include social status, security, political power, and so on. So, by focusing on religious taxes or any other source of income in general as the source of all evil in Shiʿite religious activity, they have ignored all these other important factors, and overlooked the rich and longstanding literature about the conflict of interest and its proper solution, and thus tried to reinvent the wheel.

I agree with Motahhari and Soroush that the current circumstances in religious studies in Islamic seminaries are not satisfactory. Also, I agree with them in that some of these issues are rooted in religious tax being the source of income. Nevertheless, in light of the objections that I mentioned earlier, their diagnoses and hence their solutions are problematic. In my opinion, they have failed to correctly identify the nature of the problem. The problem at hand is an instance of conflict of interest that belongs to the field of practical ethics. However, moral theorising is not enough for solving the problems of practical ethics; what we need, in addition, is a combination of various legal, cultural, educational and regulatory instruments. Putting the problem at hand in its proper place has many implications, which are, however, beyond the scope of this article. Nonetheless, and to conclude, some of these may be listed as follows:

(1) Academic misconduct is a moral problem, and like other moral problems does not have a simple solution. The most we can do is to reduce the level of misconduct. We are not able to eradicate it. Moral education is part of the solution; another part is to create an economic, social, political environment that weakens the motive for misconduct. Also, the existence of an independent

regulatory body is a necessary part of any solution.

Of course, by itself, a regulatory body is not sufficient for completely eliminating the possibility of the conflict of interest, because this body itself consists of human agents, and they themselves are vulnerable to conflict of interest. However, in tandem with other partial solutions, such as moral education, financial transparency, openness to critical review and mechanisms for professional accountability, we can hope to reduce the impact of non-epistemic factors on the process and result of one's research and study.

(2) When discussing conflict of interest we should distinguish between *immediate* and *ultimate* concerns or interests. Conflict of interest occurs when one has to choose between two immediate or two ultimate concerns that are mutually exclusive. In scholarly endeavours, to be objective and honest means that one's *immediate* concern should be to find the truth as it is and to reveal it to others, no matter what one's *ultimate* concern is. For example, one may be interested in pleasing God or reducing human suffering or even making money in searching for the truth and revealing it to others. If pleasing God or making money is one's *ultimate* concern and searching for the truth and revealing it to others one's *immediate* concern, then there is no conflict at all.

(3) From a moral point of view, we have to distinguish between two cases of conflict of interest. The first is when one of the mutually exclusive interests is immoral in itself, or it becomes immoral in the context of conflict. The second is when both mutually exclusive interests are morally significant. For example, when revealing the truth puts innocent lives, including the researcher's life, in danger. Here, the moral obligation to be honest is in conflict with the moral obligation to save innocent lives, and the former obligation is overridden by the latter. The same is true when revealing the truth increases the suffering of the audience hearing that truth so that the price they would pay for knowing that truth is too high. In such a case, one would not have the obligation to reveal the truth. In one of his interesting articles, Mostafa Malekian talks about two conflicting moral obligations that intellectuals carry, namely, revealing the truth and reducing suffering.[35] He calls this a tragic aspect of intellectual life.

(4) Sometimes the conflict is between two moral obligations that we have concerning two different aspects of religion. These are 'religion as a source of truth' and 'religion as a source of identity'. Here again it is not clear that the moral obligation of religious scholars to reveal the truth should always override

35 See M. Malekian, 'Tāghrire Ḥāghighāt va Tāghlile Mararāt: Vaghe Akhlaghi va Tragic Zendeghiye Roshanfekri', *Aftab* 13 (2002): 44–47.

their moral obligation to protect the religious identity of their community. Radical and revolutionary reforms in religious beliefs and practices under the banner of revealing the truth can put people's religious identity at risk. For many people, religion is the primary, and sometimes the only, source of moral motivation, so that their religious and moral identity overlap to a great extent. Thus, loss of religious identity can lead to a weakening of moral identity and commitment, and eventually to loss of social cohesion, and the result would be social collapse. Therefore, one may say that religious scholars should try to strike a proper balance between revealing religious truths to their audiences, on the one hand, and preserving the religious identity of their community, on the other.

JAFFER LADAK

Reviving *Ta'līf*: Strategic Charity to Counter the Rise of the Far Right

Ta'līf is one of eight categories of *ṣadaqa* mentioned in the Qur'anic verse to 'unite the hearts' (9:60) between its giver and those whom this charity reaches, the purpose of which is to either reduce enmity of potential antagonists or bring recipients closer to Islamic ideals.

In an era of a resurgent far right and the 'Islamophobia industry', the social costs of increasing fear, antagonism and discord on the basis of religious persuasion or ethnicity requires a re-examination of the strategic role of charitable services in Islam. Owing to the sheer number of global humanitarian crises, Islamic dues are often exhausted in responding to urgent relief work with micro-financing typical of strategic spending. Despite its prominence in Islamic history, *ta'līf* appears to be under-utilised, with no mainstream UK Muslim charity proposing a clear strategic application under local sociopolitical circumstances.

Ta'līf may also be understood in the realm of UK Muslim integration. Despite the trope of immigrants and Muslims in particular failing to assimilate, the Muslim Council of Britain's 'Our Shared British Future: Muslims and Integration in the UK' report suggests otherwise. Of the two million UK Muslims, 47 per cent were born in the country, 73 per cent are proud to state that their national identity is British, while 89 per cent thought 'their local area is a place where people from different backgrounds get on well'. Why, then, is there a need for UK Muslim strategic spending towards the far right? Enmity of Muslims is on the rise: 31 per cent of young children think Muslims are taking over England[1] while 37 per cent of Brits would support a political party that would reduce the number of Muslims in the UK.[2] This suggests an intergenerational problem of animosity towards the Muslim community, which requires an adequate response.

1 M. Taylor, 'Racist and Anti-immigration Views Held by Children Revealed in Schools Study', *The Guardian*, 19 May 2015, www.theguardian.com/education/2015/may/19/most-children-think-immigrants-are-stealing-jobs-schools-study-shows.

2 M. Townsend, 'Voters More Likely to Back an Anti-Muslim Party than Reject It – Poll', *The Guardian*, 16 September 2012, www.theguardian.com/uk/2012/sep/16/voters-support-anti-immigrant-party.

The Muslim community, though the most charitable in the UK, tends to export its charitable services abroad, leaving its fellow Brits unaware of their generous nature or unaccommodated for. The Muslim Charities Forum, for example, reports British Muslims give £371 per person per year to charity, with those of Jewish faith donating £270, Protestants £202, Catholics £178 and atheists £116, respectively. And while £130 million was raised in the month of Ramadan alone in 2018 by British Muslims, or £38 per second, this was spread across forty countries. Muslim impact on localised needs is, therefore, minimal. This prompted Adeem Younis, head of leading UK Muslim charity Penny Appeal to write, 'Muslims are silent about their contribution to society. It's time to drown out Islamophobes. Muslims need to better highlight their incredible humanitarian efforts at home; serving not just the vulnerable in Gaza but Gateshead too, saving lives in Syria and serving the homeless in Scarborough as well.'[3]

In response, this paper presents three avenues of exploration: the first is to draw together the evidences of *ta'līf*. This will include narrations and scholarly opinions from the Shīʿī tradition. Most importantly is a *tadabbur mawḍūʿī* – or thematic methodological – question from the Qur'an, asking, 'What is the relationship between charitable services and strategic outcomes?' These will demonstrate that there is a broad consensus on the definitions and parameters of *ta'līf* but also a distinct openness in its applicability.

The second is to highlight the socio-economic situation in the UK. In light of a decade of government-led austerity, social services and welfare programmes have drastically declined leaving 3.7 million children in poverty. Particularly challenging has been the case of hunger, with many charitable and civil society movements responding to alleviate child hunger and homelessness. This demonstrates a sphere where *ta'līf* may be applied within, proposing the example of alleviating hunger of the 'white working-class' children that may be prone to Islamophobic tropes as a strategically targeted demographic. It would follow that through Muslim charitable services towards them misunderstandings may be reduced or a 'uniting of the hearts' may occur. This would then assist in integration polemics and bringing others towards Islamic ideals.

Third is the moral epistemological question of whether charitable spending should be undertaken with a strategic purpose, such as proselytisation or reduction of enmity, or what may fall under consequentialism. Raventós and

3 A. Younis, 'Muslims Are Silent about Their Contribution to Society: It's Time to Drown Out Islamophobes', *Euro News*, 21 May 2019, www.euronews.com/2019/05/21/muslims-are-silent-about-their-contribution-to-society-it-s-time-to-drown-out-islamophobes.

Wark heavily critique the sociopolitical functions of charity, first as a means of reaffirming systemic poverty, and secondly as an effacing of the receiver's rights, stating, 'Surely respecting the dignity of those in need means honoring their capacity to decide and choose, and respecting their freedom. The focus tends, as usual, to be on the intentions of the giver without a thought as to how the receiver is affected and, still less ... how charity or philanthropy fits into the system which creates needy receivers and keeps them in that position. Nothing to do with rights.'[4] How, then, does *ta'līf* reconcile the problem of consequential charity as opposed to charitable services, irrespective of demographic or agenda? Is it an Islamic solution to social problems akin to 'pious neoliberalism' as argued by Mona Atia,[5] or does the assumption of God's supreme pleasure, as the ultimate objective of the charity, negate the consequentialism inherent in *ta'līf*?

This paper will ask whether *ta'līf* should be applied in the modern UK, and if so, where it might be deployed. It will be argued that *ta'līf*, so long as undertaken purely for the pleasure of God, is still applicable and can avoid the moral pitfall of consequentialism.

1. *Ta'līf* in the Qur'an

The triliteral root of *hamza*, *lām* and *fā'* occurs twenty-two times in the Qur'an, in four derived forms: five times in the verb *allafa*; fourteen times as the noun *alf*; once as the passive particle *mu'allafāt*; and twice as the verbal noun *īlāf*. As a verb it is used to mean 'to join or to reconcile' whilst in the passive form means 'the one who is inclined', and as a verbal noun to 'familiarise' or 'secure'.

The primary verse (9:60) employs the passive form indicating there exists a specific group of people who are either inclined, or potentially inclined, towards Islam and that charity or charitable services should be spent on them to assist their inclination. The verse states, 'Charity is meant only for the [1] poor and the [2] needy, and [3] those who are in charge thereof, and [4] those whose hearts are inclined to be won over, and for the [5] freeing of human beings from bondage, and [for] [6] those who are over burdened with debts, [7] and [for every struggle] in God's cause, and [for] [8] the wayfarer: [this is]

4 D. Raventós and J. Wark, *Against Charity* (Chico, CA: AK Press, 2018), 168.

5 M. Atia, '"A Way to Paradise": Pious Neoliberalism, Islam, and Faith-Based Development', *Annals of the Association of American Geographers* 102, no. 4 (2012): 808–27, https://doi.org/10.1080/00045608.2011.627046.

an ordinance from God – and God is all-knowing, wise.' The internal context of the verse, or *siyāq*, suggests a non-binding command as to the parameters of charitable services but also inherently there exists a deeper wisdom behind these classifications. That is to say, these specific groups have been mentioned purposefully, but not exclusively. For example, charitable services may be rendered to those needing financial aid in getting married, such as Qur'an 24:33, yet has not been mentioned within the context of God's wisdom in spending on these classifications. Spending on them would then produce the effects as per following God's unending knowledge and unerring wisdom.

From another perspective, seven of the categories appear as normative places for charitable donation; others specifically mentioned elsewhere in the Qur'an would be orphans or non-remitted loans (*qarḍ al-ḥasana*) – also normative. *Ta'līf*, however, intuitively appears distinct in it having a strategic or politicised element beyond the purely humanitarian or 'deserving' needy. This is because providing charitable services to those who may incline to Islam after receiving charity suggests a means of proselytisation.

Given that *ta'līf* is not mentioned directly in any other verse of the Qur'an suggests its initial understanding is derived from this verse and its *siyāq*. This is in conflict with a *tadabbur mawḍū'ī* or thematic approach gathering all related verses which yield both a broader picture and its nuances regarding the subject matter, much like the correct arranging of a jigsaw puzzle. What follows is a series of verses and brief analysis on the question 'What is the relationship between charitable services and strategic spending in the Qur'an?' with emphasis on its indication towards *ta'līf* as an example of strategic spending and amelioration of ties.

1.1 A *Tadabbur Mawḍū'ī* Approach to *Ta'līf*

(1) Wealth distribution is not to remain amongst one class of people but circulated as widely as possible.

> Whatever Allah has restored to His Messenger from the people of the towns, it is for Allah and for the Messenger, and for the near of kin and the orphans and the needy and the wayfarer, so that it may not be a thing taken by turns among the rich of you. (59:7)

(2) Reforming ties may be done through correct expenditure of spoils of war.

> They ask you about the spoils of war. Say: 'All spoils of war belong to God and the Messenger.' Remain, then, conscious of God, and make good the bonds of brotherhood among yourselves, and pay heed unto God and His Messenger, if you are [truly] believers! (8:1)

(3) Turning the hostile into a friend.

> Not equal are the good deed and the bad deed. Repel evil by that which is better, and then the one who is hostile to you will become as a devoted friend. But none is granted it except those who are patient and none is granted it except one having a great fortune. (41:34–35)

(4) Spending in secret and public to amend matters.

> Those who are patient, seeking the countenance of their Lord, and establish prayer and spend from what We have provided for them, secretly and publicly, and repel evil with good, for those will have the good end. (13:22)

(5) Repelling evil by spending.

> Those will be given their reward twice for what they patiently endured and they repel evil with good, and they spend from what We have provided them. (28:54)

(6) Spend in charity whilst restraining one's anger and doing good.

> They are those who spend in charity during ease and hardship and who restrain their anger and pardon the people, for God loves those who are good. (3:134)

(7) Patience and reliance on God is the response towards those who seek to harm the Muslim. Guidance has come to Muslims as it may come to their antagonists.

> And upon God let the believers rely. Why should we not rely upon God while He has guided us to our ways? We will surely be patient against whatever harm you cause us, and let them depend upon God those who would rely. (14:11–12)

(8) Charity goes to the near neighbour before the distant neighbour.

> And serve Allah and do not associate anything with Him and be good to the parents and to the near of kin and the orphans and the needy and the near neighbour and the distant neighbour ... (4:36)

(9) Address your antagonister mildly for then they may rethink their position

> But speak unto him in a mild manner, so that he might bethink himself or [at least] be filled with apprehension. (20:44)

Thematically we observe from these verses that there exists a clear relationship between charity and reform, at least in attitude if not sincerity. There is a distinct notion of changing evil to good or enmity to proximity. There is also a sense of giving to those locally before those abroad, which refers to Younis's emphasis above on the need to provide for UK-based causes to cultivate awareness of Muslim charitableness and care for local concerns.

As we will see in the next section, white working-class regions have been amongst the most disadvantaged by austerity. The verses also refer to ensuring wealth does not remain within a particular class but is spread as widely as possible. We also find the permissibility of publicising one's charity. Whilst this is usually understood as a means to encourage others or ensure awareness, to spend 'publicly' is mentioned in the absolute (*muṭlaq*) sense, without further qualification, and thus may potentially include any reasonable purpose. Joined, then, with the verse of *ta'līf*, which instinctively suggests a politicisation of one's purpose, when made public, it would enhance the likelihood of achieving the aims of *ta'līf* such as proselytisation of those inclined to Islam.

None of these verses, however, refer to *ta'līf* but rather are in the general sense referring to either principles of a political economy or humanitarianism. One may choose to add verse 9:60, and therefore include *ta'līf*, to the list of verses. It may also be possible to consider *ta'līf* as the primary subject and such verses as an expansion on its aims, guidance on how to apply it and principles on ambiguous areas, such as publicity and boundaries, for ensuring it is not abused. This denotes a profound shift in methodology, for traditionally such questions are referred to in narrations or legal principles to expound upon the primary verse. In this approach the verses of the Qur'an explain the primary verse by establishing its nuances and parameters. Narrations must then be in line with the explanatory verses set out by the Qur'an and not the other way round, or are supporting evidences for either universal or particular application as per the individual narration. Of the three methodologies, all verses being seen in conjunction with each other, the list of verses explaining the primary verse or the initial verse being explained by narrations, the first is preferred as at this juncture the question is at its broadest about strategic spending generally and how the Qur'an speaks of it, not *ta'līf* in its narrowest sense.

What is important here is that the verse regarding *ta'līf*, if taken in isolation, suggests in the very least a politicisation of charitable services; a goal other than giving for the sake of giving. When either adjoined with or explained by an array of supporting verses, it can be seen that 'doing good' or 'spending' may be undertaken with a goal of general reform. *Ta'līf* appears to speak to a particular type of reform and that is the one 'inclined' or 'potentially inclined' to Islam.

With these distinctions in mind as explanations for the application of *ta'līf*, let us review some of the narrations regarding it. These will provide understanding of its application in particular circumstances.

1.1 *Ta'līf* in *Ḥadīth* Literature

— *Ḥadīth 1: Purpose and Event of Revelation*

In a *ṣaḥīh* (rigorously authenticated) or *ḥasan* (sound) narration from Zurāra, Imām al-Bāqir was asked about the words of God regarding *ta'līf*, and said:

> They are a community testifying to God's oneness and left worship of other than God. They bore witness there is no god but God and Muhammad is the Messenger of God but they doubted in some of what he came with. So God commanded His prophet to help them incline through wealth and obedience thereby improving their Islam and establishing upon them their religion which they entered and practised. On the Day of Ḥunayn the Messenger helped incline the Arab leaders of the Quraysh; the hostile amongst them, Abū Sufyān, 'Uyayna ibn Ḥiṣn and their like.
>
> The Anṣār became angry at this and gathered around Sa'd ibn 'Ubāda, who proceeded with them to the Messenger and said, 'O Messenger of God, do you permit me to speak?' He replied, 'Yes.' He [Sa'd] said, 'If this command regarding the wealth which you divided between your community is something revealed by God, then we are pleased with it, but if it is not the case, we are not accepting of it.' The Prophet asked the Anṣār, 'Is this your collective position, as per your representative, Sa'd?'

> They replied, 'Our master is God and His Messenger'; however, another admitted, 'It is true, we are with what he said and his opinion.' So God revealed the verse and ordained *ta'līf* as part of the Qur'an.[6]

— *Ḥadīth 2: Ta'līf Is for Every Era*

> Ja'far ibn Muḥammad said, regarding *ta'līf*, 'It is for the heads of the tribes from the community who would incline towards Islam. The Prophet gave to them for the purpose of bringing them closer. And it is supposed to be used thus, in every era, if required that the divine Imām should do so.'[7]

— *Ḥadīth 3: The Condition of Giving to Those Who Are 'Known'*

> In a *ṣaḥīḥ* narration from Zurāra and Muḥammad (ibn Muslim) they said to Imām al-Bāqir, 'What is your opinion about the words of God 'Verily the *ṣadaqāt* ...' in that each of the categories are to be given even in the case that they are not known?' He replied, 'The Imām gives to them all because they owe to him obedience.' Zurāra asked, 'And if they are unknown?' The Imām responded, 'O Zurāra, if the deserved recipient is unknown to the giver, there isn't an issue for him to have to give, but rather he should give it to the one who does not know he has an active desire in religion so as to make him firm in it. In these days, do not give it, you and your companions, except to who is known. For whoever you find from amongst those deserving Muslims give to him over everyone else.' Then the Imām said, 'A part is for *ta'līf*, a part is for freeing slaves and the rest is specific.'[8]

---

6 M. Ḥ. al-Najafī, *Jawāhir al-kalām fī thawbihi al-jadīd* (Qom: Mu'assasat Dā'irat Ma'ārif al-Fiqh al-Islāmī, 2008), 8:268–69.

7 Ibid., 270.

8 Ibid.

1.2 Analysis

These narrations add detail through their specificity. In the first narration, the Prophet Muhammad gave to those who were known to be amongst his greatest of antagonisers to the initial objection of his Companions. As per verse 9:60, there exists a wisdom to this which appears to be enunciated in the words 'to help them incline through wealth and obedience thereby improving their Islam and establishing upon them their religion which they entered'. This provides clarity on who may be included in the term those 'inclined' to incorporate those who may have been ardent enemies, new converts or those who remain suspected of weak or little faith. Abū Sufyān was by this period a convert, hence 'improving their Islam ... which they entered' meaning 'to incline the heart' even of fellow Muslims. It is also important to note that the Companions did not see the wisdom in this initially but that revelation needed to inform them of it, suggesting such a practice was either not obvious to them or not current in wider society.

The second narration emphasises that *ta'līf* is to be aimed at leadership. This specification suggests that the ordinary person need not be targeted because if the head of the tribe inclines then so too would his tribe. This presupposes the structure of society remain tribal, which is not the case in the UK. One could argue that with partisanship similar patronages are built; however, the formal tribal mentality of subordination or blind following is not present in the UK and so this stipulation is not binding. The other is the statement of its practice in every era. This suggests there will always be a need for *ta'līf* and so, with the stipulation of its spending on tribal leadership removed, means that its applicability must be in accordance with time and place. It would follow that in the absence of a (divine) Imām it falls upon the scholars at their localised level to implement its spending.

The final narration refers to the relationship between the Imām and his followers in that he gives to them because they owe him obedience, which highlights his relationship of responsibility towards the eight classifications. The narration centres around those who are known and unknown for needing charitable aid. In its particular context, 'known' appears to mean 'known to be partisans of al-Bāqir'. However, there appears to be another definition of 'known' and 'unknown' in the text, which is he 'who does not know he has an active desire in religion so as to make him firm in it'. This indicates towards a person whom an observer sees in him the potential of Islam but the person is yet to realise it; spending on him may bring about this realisation. This would then mean *ta'līf* is also for the non-Muslim who might incline towards Islam if given access to do so.

In summary, two distinct definitions of those who incline are gleaned: weak-hearted Muslims who need strengthening, and the non-Muslim who may be inclined to Islam. It may also be understood that *ta'līf* is not restricted to a class of people such as the elite, political or scholarly leadership, and that it must be applied in each era.

With the principles provided by the *tadabbur mawḍūʿī* approach on how spending causes reform, and the narrations providing definitions of the meaning of 'those who incline', we now observe opinions of Shīʿī scholars from the early and contemporary periods. What will be demonstrated is that there is a broad consensus from amongst the scholars as to the definitions and recipients of *ta'līf.*

1.3 *Ta'līf* in the Opinions of the Jurisconsults (*Fuqahā'*)

— *The Opinions of Sheikh al-Ṭūsī*

> (a) [It is for] them, the disbelievers, who aspire to Islam and to unite the hearts by aiding them in the struggle of Islam towards them from it [*ta'līf*].[9]
>
> (b) [It is for] them, the community of disbelievers, who incline to Islam and to aid by them in fighting the enemy.[10]
>
> (c) [It is for] those who aspire, from amongst the disbelievers, aid from them in fighting others like them [the disbelievers].[11]

— *The Opinion of Sayyid ibn Zuhra*

> Uniting the hearts (*ta'līf*) is for those who aspire to war without there being a difference of opinion.[12]

9 Ibid., 267.
10 Ibid., 268.
11 Ibid.
12 Ibid.

– *The Opinions of Sheikh al-Mufīd*

(a) Apparently or clearly, it refers to Muslims and disbelievers.[13]

(b) They have entered into the faith but at face value there is a fear about them separating or leaving it. So they are to be united in faith justly from the tax so as to heal their hearts from what happened to them and help them to be upstanding.[14]

– *The Opinion of Muḥammad Ḥusayn al-Najafī* (*Ṣāḥib al-Jawāhir*)

Without doubt *ta'līf* is the right of everyone, in that 'uniting the hearts' [was undertaken] in the era of the Prophet, who gave *zakāt* and extra funds to those who were apparently disbelievers. And also weak-hearted but ennobled Muslims from their tribes, such as Abū Sufyān and al-Aqra' ibn Ḥābis, and others who are detailed by the scholars.

There is no difference of opinion that *ta'līf* is generally for disbelievers, those who it is intended for, unifying them for the purposes of need during war or faith in Islam; and the weak-hearted or Muslims weak of faith. This is because they are specially categorised in one of two ways: [1] it is apparent his intention is as per what was mentioned, and, moreover, the weak hearted would benefit from it, the notion of *ta'līf*, in the most specific sense. Just as mentioned in some of the previous texts about he who benefitted as per some of the fatwas indicating what is intended by *ta'līf* in the Qur'an, meaning he who inclines towards Islam or towards war with the Muslims. It is given to perfect the matter of uniting the hearts and aid in entering Islam. [2] As for giving to the disbelievers, those who do not apparently demonstrate the possibility of inclining their hearts, it [giving to them] is not without [its] problems and this requires reflection.

The condition in giving this financial resource is the hope of [bringing about] a positive effect in the one who receives it.[15]

13 Ibid.

14 Ibid.

15 Ibid.

— *The Opinion of Ṣaḥib 'Urwat al-Wuthqā*

> The categories of those deserving *zakāt:* The first: Faith. The disbeliever is not to be given from any of its categories. Nor the one whose belief is in opposition to the truth from amongst the Muslim groups including the downtrodden from them – except the part counted for those to have their hearts united.[16]

— *The Opinion of Ayatollah Sayyid Taqi al-Modarresi*

> *Ta'līf* is for two groups:
>
> (1) The disbeliever whose authority is polarised, to consolidate their relationship and attract their loyalty to Islam; to curtail and pushback against their wrongdoings and antagonism; or to benefit from them in specific matters such as war.
>
> (2) The weak-hearted Muslims, so as to give to them with the goal of stabilising and strengthening their relationship to the Islamic society.[17]

1.4 Analysis

The majority of statements appear to accord with the categories and higher goals established from the verses and narrations cited previously. There does also appear to be an added emphasis on those inclined to war against Islam, which suggests that the connotation of weak-heartedness need not be restricted to Muslims but those antagonisers who, if financial or otherwise benefit might reach them, would disincline towards war. This would be in keeping with the primary meaning of reducing enmity.

Two other comments are of interest. Ṣāḥīb al-Jawāhir states, 'As for giving to the disbelievers, those who do not apparently demonstrate the possibility of inclining their hearts, it [giving to them] is not without [its] problems and this requires reflection.' The apparent demonstration is entirely subjective to the observer or giver. What is the criterion here? The simple asking of a question regarding Islam, or an outright hatred that has caused him or her to research

16 M. K. Yazdi, *al-'Urwa al-wuthqā* (Qom: Mu'assasat al-Nashr al-Islāmī, 2007), 4:124.

17 M. T. al-Modarresi, *al-Wajīz fī al-fiqh al-Islāmī* (Najaf: Dār al-Maḥajja al-Bayḍā', 2014), 3:53.

Islam for the purposes of misunderstanding it? Al-Bāqir's definition to Zurāra, 'the one who does not know he has an active desire in religion', confirms the relativity but both of these are at an individual level; interestingly, no mention is made about spending on inclined people at a collective level. In either case there needs to be a reasonable expectation that the money is not simply going to be wasted.

Ṣāḥib al-Jawāhir adds, 'The condition in giving this financial resource is the hope of [bringing about] a positive effect in the one who receives it.' This, of course, cannot be measured in advance nor can its effect after spending, even more so at the collective level. This is because *ta'līf* is to 'incline the hearts', which is an internal matter. It is, as it states, in 'the hope', and that must be reasonable.

2. Applying *Ta'līf* in the UK

Various jurisconsults, countries and organisations apply *ta'līf* according to their understanding and circumstance: Dr Ruhaini Muda of Universiti Teknologi Malaysia (UTM) states that citizens who register an interest with the Malay government, such as through census forms, receive free books on Islam.[18] This would certainly meet the criterion to 'demonstrate the possibility of inclining'.

The UK, however, has no published, systematised application of *ta'līf*. The National Zakat Foundation (NZF) states amongst its goals 'assisting and strengthening Islam' to 'improve ... public perception towards Islam and Muslims' and the 'mission to distribute Zakat transformatively within the United Kingdom'.[19] Although there appears no specific recourse to appreciate how this applies to *ta'līf*, the NZF states its impact includes to 'publicly promote the praiseworthy work of Muslim leaders and organisations',[20] which may be a practical way of decreasing enmity.

In this section, I will present the general picture of the legacy of a decade of austerity on children in the UK, and specifically its impact on child hunger. Particular interest will be paid towards geographical locations of white working-class demographics, which may be suffering with food shortages. The aim, here, is to present a space for *ta'līf* to be applied, with the view of a 'reasonable' response of reducing enmity towards Islam by the targeted demographics.

---

18 7th Annual Contemporary Fiqhi Issues Workshop, Al-Mahdi Institute, 4–5 July 2019.

19 C. Stirk, 'An Act of Faith: Humanitarian Financing and Zakat', *Briefing Paper* (Bristol: Global Humanitarian Assistance, 2015).

20 National Zakat Foundation, *Our Partners*, www.nzf.org.uk/About/Partners.

2.1 Child Hunger in the UK: A Space for Applying *Ta'līf*

In a decade of austerity the number of children living in 'absolute poverty' across the UK has reached 3.7 million.[21] In ten constituencies, child poverty is above 50 per cent, with charities claiming this is now the 'new normal'.[22] Although many children services have been cut, what has seen a particular increase has been the rise of child hunger. This has been exacerbated by governmental plans to end free school meals. In response, the executive director of the Education Policy Institute, Natalie Perera, stated, 'Around 900,000 children from low-income families will lose their eligibility for free school meals under these proposals.'[23]

This has led to shocking reports about hunger and how children are responding. One mainstream newspaper headline read 'British children so hungry they eat loo paper and scavenge in bins, says charity', with Laurence Guinness, chief executive of the Childhood Trust, warning of parents being unable to feed their children over the summer without free school meals.[24] Another newspaper headline read 'Children "stealing food" and too tired to learn, Leeds' headteachers warn', in which the article quoted a headteacher stating, 'Abject poverty affects nearly all my children,' fearing that school dinners are often the only hot meal a student will have that day. 'Our children's shoes are open, clothes threadbare,' the headteacher of one Leeds primary school said. 'Our support with food bank vouchers has risen steadily over the last few years from an already high starting point. The school is working with social care colleagues to provide money for families for things like electricity and heating, they added, while teachers had stepped in to donate prams and baby clothes.'[25] Local councils are having to

21 M. Bulman, 'Number of Children in Absolute Poverty across UK Hits 3.7 Million after Increases of 200,000 in a Year', *Independent*, 28 March 2019, www.independent.co.uk/news/uk/home-news/child-poverty-absolute-uk-housing-crisis-costs-austerity-conservatives-a8843381.html.

22 P. Butler, 'Child Poverty above 50% in 10 UK Constituencies', *The Guardian*, 15 May 2019, www.theguardian.com/society/2019/may/15/child-poverty-above-50-per-cent-in-10-uk-constituencies.

23 G. Wilford, 'Almost One Million Families to Be Hit by Theresa May's Plan to End Free School Lunches, Think Tank Warns', *Independent*, 21 May 2017, www.independent.co.uk/news/uk/home-news/theresa-may-conservatives-free-school-lunches-cuts-poverty-a7747066.html.

24 L. Johnston, 'British Children So Hungry They Eat Loo Paper and Scavenge in Bins, Says Charity', *Mirror*, 18 August 2019, www.mirror.co.uk/news/uk-news/british-children-hungry-eat-loo-18957247.

25 R. Kitchen, 'Children "Stealing Food" and Too Tired to Learn, Leeds' Headteachers

step in and feed children during school holidays after research revealed that families are going hungry. One council said research suggests nearly a third of parents earning under £25,000 per annum skip meals in the holidays so their children can eat and almost two-thirds struggle to afford food at weekends and during school holidays. Groups like the Trussell Trust are struggling to cope with demand from parents and research has suggested that pressure on food banks doubles during the holidays.[26]

White working-class areas are amongst those that have been worst affected. Wales, for example, which voted to leave the EU, suggesting a dissatisfaction with immigration trends, denied children access to school services until parents had paid off school lunch debts, with forced recovery from bailiffs threatened.[27] In the north-west of England, fourteen districts from Blackpool to Lancaster all overwhelmingly voted to leave the EU, ranging from 51 to 67 per cent in favour. These trends were matched with the newly incorporated Brexit Party dominating across the same region in the subsequent elections, heavily linked to anti-immigrant and anti-Islamic sentiments. Burnley, for example, has some 8,800 children – or almost 50 per cent – living in poverty, reflecting the same hunger circumstances described above.

In the same region, as anti-immigrant sentiment grows, the far right are 'infiltrating children's charities with anti-Islam agenda'. *The Guardian* reports:

> In Rochdale, a community group for child sexual abuse survivors, Shatter Boys, said it had been approached repeatedly by senior Ukip figures including Lord Pearson, who offered to introduce them to millionaire donors and fund an open-top bus to raise the alarm about grooming gangs. Pearson's offer of funding, made during a private lunch at the House of Lords, followed months of courting by the Ukip families spokesman, Alan Craig, who last year said Muslim grooming gangs had committed a 'Holocaust of our children'. Craig said paedophilia could be traced back 'to Muhammad himself'.[28]

Warn', *Yorkshire Evening Post*, 3 May 2019, www.yorkshireeveningpost.co.uk/education/children-stealing-food-and-too-tired-learn-leeds-headteachers-warn-633416.

26 Wilfred, 'Almost One Million Families'.

27 K. Williams, 'Kids Will Be "Denied Access to Schools Services" if They Don't Pay Dinner Money Debts', *Daily Post*, 15 July 2019, www.dailypost.co.uk/news/north-wales-news/kids-denied-access-school-services-16585378.

28 J. Halliday, 'Far Right "Infiltrating Children's Charities with Anti-Islam Agenda"', *The Guardian*, 5 March 2019, www.theguardian.com/world/2019/mar/05/far-right-infil-

It is evident that several trends are converging at once: austerity, severe child poverty and hunger, anti-Muslim sentiment and far-right manipulation of the situation. It is likely, then, that the longer anti-immigrant and anti-Muslim reactions are fostered as the solution to such sociopolitical problems, the more likely such attitudes will become a generational trend. It is here that *ta'līf* with its sociopolitical goal of 'uniting the hearts' can be applied. Whilst in the traditional understanding *ta'līf* serves to reduce enmity, it may also be considered in this space as removing the perceived threat of Islam or that Muslims are simply too segregated to be aware of, or care about, the challenges falling on the white working class, indicated by Younis. This amounts to the same goal but also the need to add another clear definition to its remit.

Ta'līf would mean, for example, identifying schools or breakfast clubs, particularly in white working-class areas often prone to far-right propaganda, and providing the necessary funding or services for meals. The Muslim concern for and assistance to the children of those worst impacted would reform their attitude and 'unite' the hearts.

Providing the finances alone, however, would not be sufficient for meeting the requirements, as Ṣāḥib al-Jawāhir states, 'The condition in giving this financial resource is the hope of [bringing about] a positive effect in the one who receives it.' If the goal is to reduce enmity or incline the hearts of those with potentiality to Islam, or in this case removing a perceived threat of Islam, the recipients at least, if not their parents, peers and wider community, must be informed of who is providing the services in order to achieve its aim, such as through social or traditional media. This raises the moral question of whether it is appropriate to give charitable aid with an intention other than for its own goodness, or, in this case, an unstated sociopolitical cause or proselytisation.

3. The Moral Debate over *Ta'līf*

Consequentialism refers to the value of an act as determined by its outcome. In its moral sense, it means that the act is morally preferable if it will produce a selected outcome. This raises the question as to whether charity should be bestowed for the purpose of a personally preferable outcome, the opposite of which suggests that if that outcome were not to occur, the charity would not be bestowed or regretted. In the case of *ta'līf,* this is explicated by Ṣāḥib al-Jawāhir, who states, 'As for giving to the disbelievers, those who do not appar-

---

trating-childrens-charities-with-anti-islam-agenda.

ently demonstrate the possibility of inclining their hearts, it [giving to them] is not without [its] problems and this requires reflection,' thus those who are not determined to potentially incline may not be given this specific financial resource, though it does not necessarily prohibit them from receiving another type of financial aid from Islamic dues.

Most forms of Islamic charitable aids appear without such conditionality; some Qur'anic verses indicate wealth may be spent to reverse that which is spent to hinder people from God or corruption (see 8:36, 9:34 and 2:188), while another indicates that money can be spent on sex workers for the purpose of liberating them from this exploitation (24:33). These are also in the realm of consequentialism. From a moral perspective, however, would these be seen differently?

Ta'līf, moreover, appears with a specific sociopolitical aim of normalisation of Islam or its spread – a point which has not escaped criticism. Christian activists deeming themselves as protectors of Western civilisation consider *ta'līf* a form of bribery or means of buying off opposition to Islam used to eventually establish its legal system stating, 'In order to establish smooth levels of acceptability of Islamic rules and regulations even in a hostile society, Islam established a key principle: court those who are not in agreement to attempt to win them over by all means. This is done through the principle of the "Reconciliation of the Hearts".'[29]

From another perspective, if civil society subsidises basic needs, it de-incentivises the government in fulfilling its duty of providing for human rights, like sufficient access to food. Raventós and Wark emphasise this, which is also *The Guardian*'s view on impoverished schools, arguing charity is not the answer.[30] Furthermore, if an Islamic understanding of charity is not to leave its recipients as perpetual beggars but rather be a model for social empowerment, how does *ta'līf* achieve this if it leaves its recipient seeking further financial aid and not the religion itself?

In this section, I will explain some of the arguments against charitable consequentialism and explore whether *ta'līf* can be applied without appealing to religious consequentialism.

---

29 S. Solomon, 'Islamisation through Halal Products', *Christian Concern*, 8–12, https://archive.christianconcern.com/sites/default/files/20190114_ChristianConcern_PolicyReport_HalalFoods.pdf.

30 Editorial, 'The Guardian View on Impoverished Schools: Charity is Not the Answer', *The Guardian*, 16 June 2019, www.theguardian.com/commentisfree/2019/jun/16/the-guardian-view-on-impoverished-schools-charity-is-not-the-answer?utm_term=Autofeed&CMP=twt_gu&utm_medium=&utm_source=Twitter#Echobox=1560709904.

3.1 The Moral Wrongs of Consequentialism

The common element of charity should be that its distribution is not based on those deemed worthy or unworthy as determined by ideology but rather universal and from the perspective of rights, love and care for all. As Thomas Browne stated in his *Religio Midici*, 'to redress other Men's misfortunes upon the common considerations ... is a sinister and politick kind of charity'.[31] Those deemed unworthy gives rise to frustration from the non-recipient or lack of care shown to their plight, and their disenfranchisement is caused by the giver. This leads to sectarianism between the two and the guise of superiority for one deemed worthy to receive. Charity ceases to function, as its purpose of universality is not only obliterated but is now a tool for suppression of some and empowerment of the chosen few.

On the other hand, charity is by its nature a 'total social fact', which has always brought 'together tribes, clans, families and even groups from different territories'.[32] After all, benevolence breeds solidarity; otherwise, the institution of gift-giving is nullified.

In this sense charity has always taken on a sociopolitical function. Moral consequentialism would ask whether this is appropriate or befitting of a devotional service to be tainted with self-service. Bernard Mandeville's 'An Essay on Charity and Charity Schools' (1723) criticises 'respectable do-gooders whose renown comes from ... their hypocritical hiding of their private vice behind public benefit. Individuals who indulged in works for the public benefit were merely acting out of self-love'.[33] This refers to the problem of charity being doled out on the basis of the intention of the giver and not actually the needs of the receiver. It also speaks to a larger problem of intention in that his targeting for 'charity' has been based on his vulnerability, for, in the case of *ta'līf*, the greater his material need, the more likely he will see Islam as benevolent. This compounds the potential number of problems for (a) if he does not show potential of proselytisation, he should not be given, and (b) the greater his need, the more likely he is to incline, hence one should wait longer till his need is greatest. This not only exacerbates the sufferer's needs, it disregards his or her freedoms in the knowledge that when suffering greater, he or she is more likely to respond as the giver hopes. From the perspective of the giver, this

31 T. Browne, *Religio Midici* (N.p.: Pantianos Classics, 2006 [1642]), 130.

32 Raventós and Wark, *Against Charity*, 21.

33 Ibid., 164.

dehumanises the receiver until he or she feels most likely to 'incline'.

The reason for 'inclining' towards the giver is, then, misunderstood. Is it out of desperation or fear that if 'inclination' is not heeded the 'charity' will no longer be available? Or is it that what the giver is offering is not better than any other system – it is just less bad? Is it that Islam wishes to demonstrate its economic superiority by providing, where all other systems have failed to provide? Here, philanthrocapitalism is similar, where financial support is provided for the purpose of establishing capitalism as the supreme economic ideology; through its juggernaut of financial reach it creates a dependency or power-based relationship where the poor must return to the rich for their needs. One of the Rockefeller Foundation's strategic documents from 1951 demonstrates its reasoning for 'charity' as evidencing capitalism as the supreme ideology: 'Whether additional millions in Asia and elsewhere will become Communists will depend partly on whether the Communist world or the free world fulfils its promises. Hungry people are lured by promises, but they may be won by deeds. Communism makes attractive promises to the underfed peoples; democracy must not only promise as much, but must deliver more.'[34]

3.2 *Ta'līf* as Other than Consequentialism

The argument for *ta'līf* being consequentialist is possibly self-evident. It exists within its name, associated narrations and scholarly works, that its deployment is for the intent of stipulated outcomes. For brevity, consequentialism as a moral wrong has not been debated above, but rather arguments for it being wrong have been presented. Based on this assumption, *ta'līf* would also be subjected to these moral questions. One response to admitting its consequentialism is reverting to a *tadabbur mawḍūʿī* approach, a submissive outlook stating God knows better as per the Qur'anic prescription of inherent divine wisdom in this practice (9:60) or that the Prophet Muhammad acted as such.

Another response would be to deny its consequentialism and this attribution as a misunderstanding of its purpose. The Qur'anic verse that underpins all almsgivings states, 'O you who believe! Cancel not your charity by reminders of your generosity or by injury – like those who spend their substance to be seen of men, but believe neither in God nor in the Last Day' (2:264). Amongst these injuries that invalidate charity is for its intention to be for other than the sake

34 R. Patel, 'The Long Green Revolution', *The Journal of Peasant Studies* 40, no. 1 (2012): 11, https://doi.org/10.1080/03066150.2012.719224.

of God, including any pragmatist purpose. Why should *ta'līf* be an exception? In fact, any charitable giving has been inherently linked with worldly benefits. Narrations such as 'Charity repels tribulation and calamity',[35] 'When you become penniless then do business with God through charity',[36] 'Charity given in secret expiates wrongdoings and charity given openly is a means of increasing wealth'[37] and 'Charity protects'[38] all speak to metaphysical advantages, yet despite knowing these, the verse prohibits giving for these outcomes, or at least the degree with which it is given for said sake injures the pure intent to the same extent. This would suggest that there exists a balance between consciousness of outcomes in choosing when, where and how to deploy charity whilst its intention still being purely for the sake of God. Where, then, is the reconciliation? The worldly outcome is not the goal but a non-incidental benefit. The benefit is still in the hands of God and so whether it occurs or not is neither in the control of the giver nor in the expectation. Moreover, its occurrence is only beneficial to the degree in which God permits and so there is no disappointment in its non-occurrence but rather a greater blessing. This would mean that *ta'līf* is not an exception but rather the norm as with any other charitable service. It is to be undertaken purely for the sake of God with knowledge that it brings about a particular benefit. This would also prohibit the dehumanisation of the recipient, for if not deemed appropriate to be given through *ta'līf*, it would certainly fall into one of the other categories in Qur'an 9:60.

What is interesting in the realm of distinguishing the worthy is that the narrations regarding *ta'līf* appear to target the tribal leaders, those who were previously wealthy elites of their community or even criminally antagonistic towards Islam, such as Abū Sufyān, and not the poor as those deemed worthy, who are suggested as contemporary recipients in the second section of this article above. As the pagans departed en masse from Abū Sufyān, he would have been boycotted and suffered from indignation and, upon entry to Islam, ostracisation. Islam, unlike Marxism, does not consider wealth or the wealthy to be inherently problematic nor does it set up a rivalry between the poor and rich or owners and workers. Islam saw no need to punish the newly converted Abū Sufyān by reducing his esteem or social status or, by his known history

35 A. W. al-Tamīmī, *Ghurar al-ḥikam wa-durar al-kalim* (Beirut: Mu'assasat al-A'lami li-l-Maṭbū'āt, 2002), 175.

36 Ibid.

37 Ibid.

38 Ibid.

of antagonism, keep him at a distance or in an outer circle of stigmatised or censured believers. As the Qur'an says twice, 'I do not revile the believers' (11:29 and 26:114). From this perspective, it is appropriate to suggest that the *ta'līf* lavished upon him was not to purchase his loyalty but rather to help return his dignity and social status, without which, Abū Sufyān would have always considered himself in a state of loss because of Islam and be perceived as an 'outsider' in a moral economy which prided itself on early conversion and its giving for the sake of Islam; Abū Sufyān would have had neither and little chance of making up the latter.

Political economy understands spending as a means of reducing marginalisation: Karl Marx admitted, 'the exchange of commodities evolves originally not within primitive communities but on their margins, on their borders, the few points where they come into contact with other communities.'[39]

Donald Pfaff explains this in an influential study, 'The Altruistic Brain: How We Are Naturally Good', that the human brain is 'wired' to do good. This is based on evolutionary survival, which relies on caring for the welfare of others and seeing their needs through the image of our own needs. This would suggest that the degree to which a person requires resource, dignity and rights, is commensurate with how he or she sees the same need for others. Providing it to others, then, is no more selfish than demanding it for oneself. From a social perspective, a marginalised individual wishes to be treated normally or understood and therefore also wishes this for those 'othered'. Pfaff states that charitable services can be 'deployed to help bring antisocial individuals into the mainstream'. Raventós and Wark dismiss the value of this, asking what type of 'mainstream' do they want to bring people into, where social engineering and identity removal have been hallmarks of history.[40]

Whilst that critique is correct, *ta'līf* which is purely for the pleasure of God need not be seen through the lens of subtle coercion but rather a restoration of the basic right of dignity. The consequence is not the goal but a benefit. The very claim of charity being non-distinguishing needs to be challenged here to be understood, for in order to give, the recipient must be identified in the first place by some criteria. If the criteria includes (a) understanding relative social norms and (b) a return to dignity within those norms, *ta'līf* was spent on those deemed to have had their social dignity stripped from them and, through

39 K. Marx, *A Contribution to the Critique of Political Economy, Part I* (Charleston, SC: BiblioLife, 2009 [1859]), 54.

40 Raventós and Wark, *Against Charity*, 55–59.

expenditure, aids them to a return of it. This would not, then, be seeking inclining to Islam in the quid pro quo sense of consequentialism, but rather through an understanding that Islam cared for their dignity and so they would incline to a religion that protected their social rights, even if it be an arch-antagonist such as Abū Sufyān.

CONCLUSION

Ta'līf is part of the Islamic economy of giving. Despite being overtly mentioned in the Qur'an and *ḥadīth* literature it appears to have been neglected in the UK, at least as a systemically applied principle or strategic consideration for responding to the rise of anti-Muslim sentiment. This is surprising given the present political atmosphere and violent ramifications upon the Muslim community.

Strategic spending, or a non-short-sighted good undertaken with knowledge of its positive effect, is a wide subject matter within the Qur'an. Given that *ta'līf*, or charitable spending, is one form of good, it must be seen within that topic and speaks to a wider human principle of relieving misunderstandings between people, and that human interaction is appreciative and even reciprocal in matters of goodwill. Thus, *ta'līf* enters the domain of competing visions of the poor and rich. It may be understood as an act for the sake of purchasing loyalty and proximity or as part of a wider moral economy that understands relationships are not always mutual, and that doing good to others is a means of winning their hearts and defeating ignorance in a normative sense. Indeed, amongst the Qur'anic reasonings for existence is to get to know one another (49:13). This may occur through gift-giving or awareness of another's circumstances and being of assistance.

Amira Mittermaier, a scholar of the Egyptian revolution and the role charitable services played in influencing socio-religious and sociopolitical positioning, as well as the reconstruction of the country, argues a third, more accurate perspective; namely, that a truly Islamic logic of giving disrupts secular, liberal or Christian notions of giving, something that attempts to pervert the understanding of *ta'līf* altogether. Mittermaier asks, how does the ethics of a God-centric giving erase the consequentialism of alms giving? She describes 'a triadic logic of giving' where there is always the donor recipient and God in the picture, which is inescapable when giving in the name of religion; at times this relationship takes a more trade-like form where the poor are quite literally used as a medium for interacting with God or trading with God, or something that is closer to the donor raising him or herself to becoming the medium, in a sense that the donor embodies divine generosity or God's hand. However, Mittermaier argues that the focus on compassion and identity is a 'key ethos of our time, a secularised version of a Christian emphasis on compassion which increasingly replaces a logic of rights'.[41] The God-oriented charity sees the act of giving as not placing the charity in the hands of the recipient but actually in the hands of God Himself, metaphorically speaking. This removes the ethical dilemma of consequentialism as neither is any outcome sought other than God's pleasure, nor is any known potential outcome in one's own hands – it is now 'in the hands of God', so to speak. This suggests Islamic ethics needs not fall into the trap of a secularised understanding of Christian compassion or a selective choice in relieving suffering, what Didier Fassin calls 'humanitarian reasoning'.[42]

The narrations and scholarly commentary appear not to speak at length on its application across time and space. They specify targeting tribal leadership, which has a very narrow reach, but this also refers to a particular paradigm. Given that textual sources speak in principled terms, this allows for a much wider scope of its usage. This flexibility is needed when considering nuances between communities in removing misunderstandings or providing what may often be covert or sensitive applications.

British children, particularly those of a white working-class background, more prone to anti-immigrant and anti-Muslim rhetoric, are equally being hit hardest by a right-wing government austerity plan. Though charitable services should be afforded to them irrespective of background, wisdom dictates there being a pragmatic opportunity to present a side of Islam that they may not have yet encountered. That is, one of awareness, care and fighting on their behalf for a better opportunity in life. It is only normal that those who might not have considered Islamic laws or Muslim populations, also riddled with the same economic woes, to have these concerns for them to reimagine their stances towards Islam. If, then, promoting the charitable services provided to children of these demographics reaches their parents and communities, it is reasonable to imagine that more than one generation of antagonists may be positively affected.

41 S. Tareen, 'Amira Mittermaier, "Giving to God: Islamic Charity in Revolutionary Times" (U California Press, 2019)', *New Books Network*, 11 June 2019, podcast, https://newbooksnetwork.com/amira-mittermaier-giving-to-god-islamic-charity-in-revolutionary-times-u-california-press-2019/amp/?__twitter_impression=true. For further reading, see A. Mittermaier, *Giving to God: Islamic Charity in Revolutionary Times* (Berkeley, CA: University of California Press, 2019).

42 See D. Fassin, *Humanitarian Reason: A Moral History of the Present* (Berkeley, CA: University of California Press, 2013).

Anti-Muslim propaganda, especially analysis of Islam's sociopolitical presence, has become the norm. This means a great degree of scepticism towards Muslim public life. *Ta'līf* with the intent of buying loyalty or reducing enmity would only exacerbate such suspicions. This undermines any potential *ta'līf* has and so cannot be a wise instruction as per the primary verse (9:60). It would follow that *ta'līf* is undertaken not for the intent of a sociopolitical outcome but rather that God's wisdom lies in this, trust in His knowledge of its effect and His pleasure are the reasons for its bestowal. This does not contradict the knowledge that its spending may bring about felicity between groups.

Given that it is a clear Qur'anic instruction, *ta'līf* can no longer be ignored. Its application by a relatively new Muslim community, as a minority, in a secular state, during intense socio-religious tensions is starkly different to its application during its revelation. It would be tempting to apply it with targeted modes of advertising and measurement so as to capture its effectiveness; based on the moral interpretation of knowing its real-world consequences versus leaving its outcomes to God, this may be counterproductive and sully the puritanical logic argued above.

There are clear, target demographics and opportunities in which to apply *ta'līf*, and so long as the intention is correct, should be initiated, not as a trial but with the confidence of being a means of positive social change.

Lightning Source UK Ltd.
Milton Keynes UK
UKHW020629160821
388939UK00011B/945

9 781838 032005